Pattern-Driven
Software Problem Solving
Introduction

Dmitry Vostokov
Memory Dump Analysis Services

Published by OpenTask, Republic of Ireland

OpenTask books and magazines are available through booksellers and distributors worldwide. For further information or comments send requests to press@opentask.com.

A CIP catalogue record for this book is available from the British Library.

ISBN-l3: 978-1-908043-17-7 (Paperback)

First printing, 2011

Pattern-Driven
Software Problem Solving
Introduction

Presenter: Dmitry Vostokov
Memory Dump Analysis Services

Hello Everyone! My name is Dmitry Vostokov and I'm a founder of Memory Dump Analysis Services which specializes in crash dump analysis and debugging. The topic of today's presentation is Software Problem Solving using patterns. The topic is so big that I devised a whole series of such presentations with this particular one being just an introduction.

Prerequisites

Experience in software troubleshooting and/or debugging

I assume that you already have some experience in software troubleshooting or debugging. There is something for everyone in this presentation even if you have never fixed any software defect.

Agenda (Summary)

- A Short History
- Basic Definitions
- Pattern Categories
- Future Research Directions

This is a short presentation. Instead of trying to cover everything about patterns I only provide hints and links where to find further information. I survey what I have done during the last 5 years. Because ...

... tomorrow is 5 years of DumpAnalysis.org. Originally conceived as a forum to discuss memory dump analysis issues it was later transformed into a blog, then into a portal, then it was a dream to become ForensicAnalysis.org, then it became associated with software trace analysis via TraceAnalysis.org and finally with Victimware.org.

Agenda (Basic Definitions)

- Software Problems
- Software Patterns
- DA+TA
- Pattern Hybridization

First we talk about software problems and clarify which problem category we consider for this presentation. Next we talk about software patterns and also clarify which pattern category we consider here. Then we have a look at **DA+TA** acronym and define a metaphor we call **Pattern Hybridization**.

Software Problems

- Construction: Requirements, Architecture, Design, and Implementation
- **Post-Construction: Maintenance and Support**

Problems

Construction

Requirements, Architecture, Design, and Implementation

Problems

Post-Construction

Maintenance and Support

Post-construction problem: any observed deviations in structure and behavior between modeling expectations and the actual built system.*

* What is a Software Defect?

What is a Software Defect?
http://www.dumpanalysis.org/blog/index.php/2008/01/08/what-is-a-software-defect/

Let's consider software problems. Software development engineers usually think about software problems as problems with building software (construction problems), for example, design problems. Software support engineers usually think about software problems as problems in production environments (we call it post-construction problems). The distinction is not clear cut and there is some overlap between these two categories. The typical costruction example: "How we design and build a system based on functional requirements and non-functional constraints?" The typical post-costruction example: "What we had built stopped working. How do we bring it back working?"

Software Patterns

- Construction: Requirements, Architecture, Design, and Implementation
- **Post-Construction: Maintenance and Support**

() Patterns	Patterns ()
Construction	**Post-Construction**
Requirements, Architecture, Design, and Implementation	Maintenance and Support

Pattern: a common recurrent identifiable problem together with a set of recommendations and possible solutions to apply in a specific context

We use patterns to solve problems. Here we relax the usual definition of a pattern having a definite solution. Anything works. So our definition is this: a common recurrent identifiable problem together with a set of recommendations and possible solutions to apply in a specific context. Patterns are also a part of pattern language useful for communication. Again our main focus is on post-construction patterns although we consider construction patterns for troubleshooting and debugging tools.

DA+TA

- DA: Dump Artifact / Dump Analysis

  Memory snapshots: process, kernel, physical memory dumps

- TA: Trace Artifact / Trace Analysis

  Software traces: Event Tracing for Windows, logs

By chance **DATA** looks like a good abbreviation for **D**ump **A**rtifact **A**nalysis and **T**race **A**rtifact **A**nalysis. By a dump we mean a memory snapshot usually called memory dump, crash dump, or core dump. By a trace we mean a log, for example Process Monitor logs or Citrix CDF traces which are based on Microsoft Event Tracing for Windows.

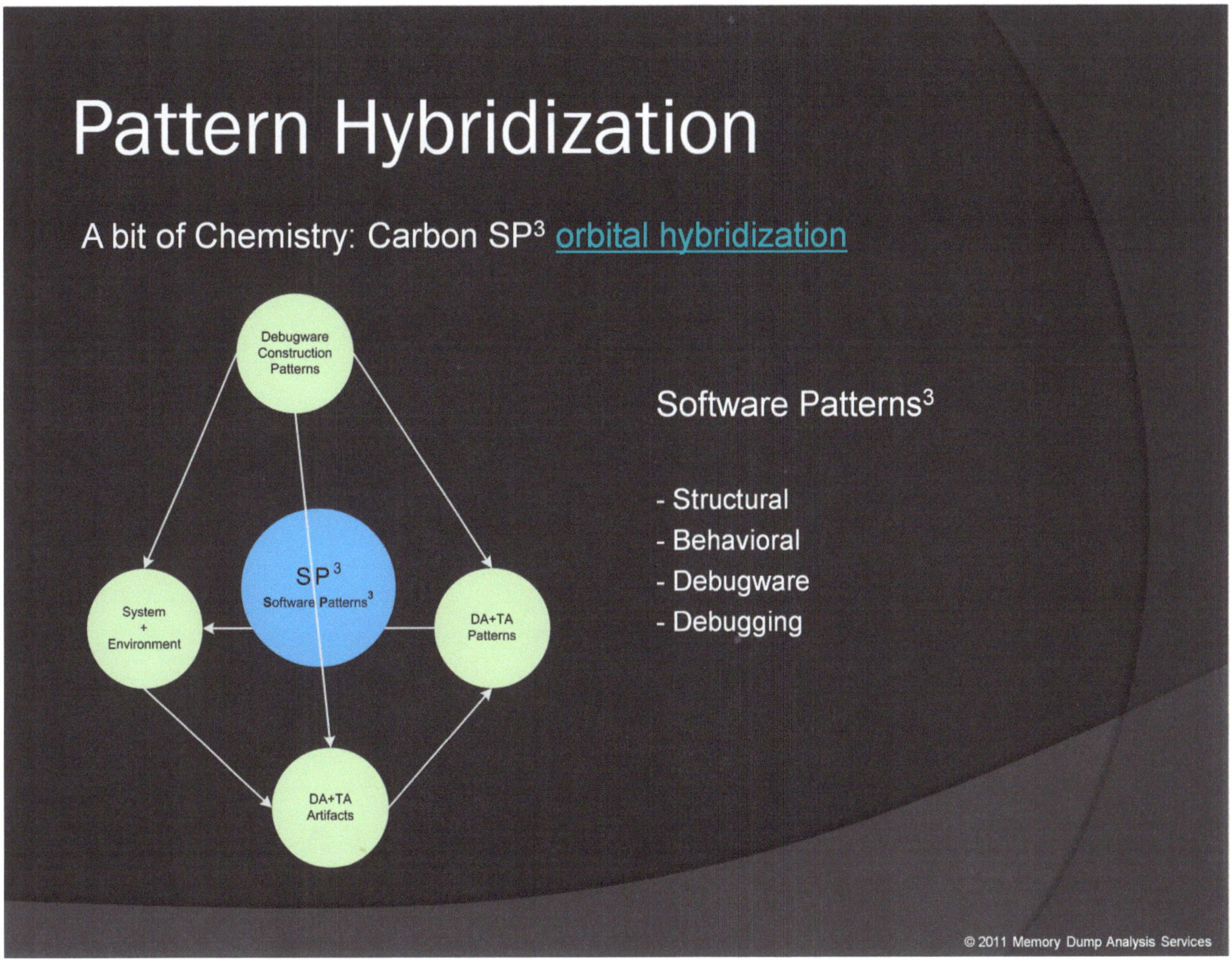

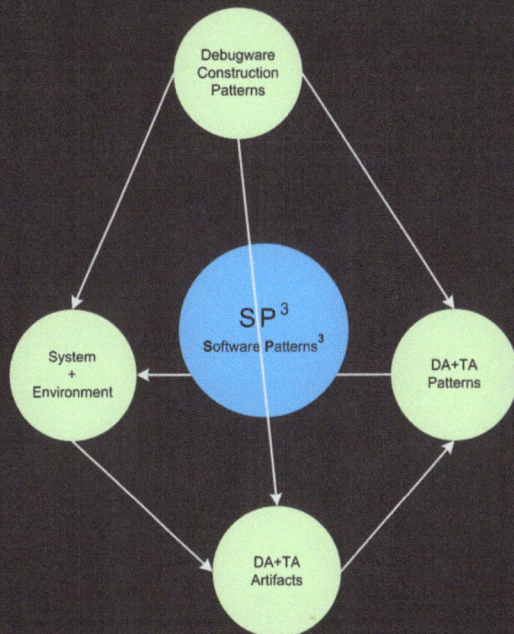

Pattern Hybridization

A bit of Chemistry: Carbon SP³ orbital hybridization

Software Patterns³

- Structural
- Behavioral
- Debugware
- Debugging

(Diagram labels: Debugware Construction Patterns; SP³ Software Patterns³; System + Environment; DA+TA Patterns; DA+TA Artifacts)

© 2011 Memory Dump Analysis Services

Orbital hybridization
http://en.wikipedia.org/wiki/Orbital_hybridisation

Now we introduce Pattern Hybridization. This is just a fancy term borrowed from Chemistry with an acronym **SP3** to name the mixture of 4 types of **S**oftware **P**atterns: Structural, Behavioral, Tools and Debugging. The diagram shows the pattern-driven process where a system and its environment provide DATA artifacts which we analyze and recognize DATA patterns in them. The results are used to alter the system and its environment. All these stages are facilitated by patterns for troubleshooting and debugging tools which we call **Debugware** patterns. Tools are used to produce and collect artifacts, alter the system and its environment, and to recognize other patterns.

11

Now we come to the next block of slides. We consider pattern categories such as Software Behavior, Debugware, Workaround, and Unified Debugging.

Spiking Thread
http://www.dumpanalysis.org/blog/index.php/2007/05/11/crash-dump-analysis-patterns-part-14/

Discontinuity
http://www.dumpanalysis.org/blog/index.php/2009/08/04/trace-analysis-patterns-part-8/

Software behavior patterns are visible and discernible signs in memory dump and software trace artifacts as a result of analysis. Some of them are results from software defects and some are results from unanticipated and unexpected software interaction. There are lots of patterns on DumpAnalysis.org portal. The picture shows that when you go there on the left hand side you would see memory dump analysis patterns and on the right hand side you would see software trace analysis patterns. You may notice some pictures or icons on the left: this is a not yet completed project to give each pattern a pattern icon. When we finish with dump analysis patterns you would see icons on the right too.

DA: Software Behavior

- Memory dump: a memory snapshot
- Definition, partial classification and historical list
- Pattern identification case studies

© 2011 Memory Dump Analysis Services

Definition, partial classification and historical list
http://www.dumpanalysis.org/blog/index.php/crash-dump-analysis-patterns/

Pattern identification case studies
http://www.dumpanalysis.org/blog/index.php/pattern-cooperation/

This slide provides various links to memory dump analysis patterns and their case studies that you can browse when you download the presentation PDF file afterwards from this location:

http://www.dumpanalysis.com/files/Pattern-Driven-Software-Problem-Solving-Introduction.pdf

Definition, and historical list

http://www.dumpanalysis.org/blog/index.php/trace-analysis-patterns/

Pattern identification case studies

http://www.dumpanalysis.org/blog/index.php/pattern-cooperation/

Similar links are available for software trace analysis patterns and their case studies. Actually there are parallels between some software trace patterns and memory dump patterns. For example, stack traces can be analyzed using some trace analysis patterns. The patterns we propose are general and not tied to a specific product. Because I used to analyze software traces with millions of lines and with messages from hundreds of components where most of them were completely unfamiliar for me (and I had never seen underlying source code) I proposed very general ones that can be used even for network traces.

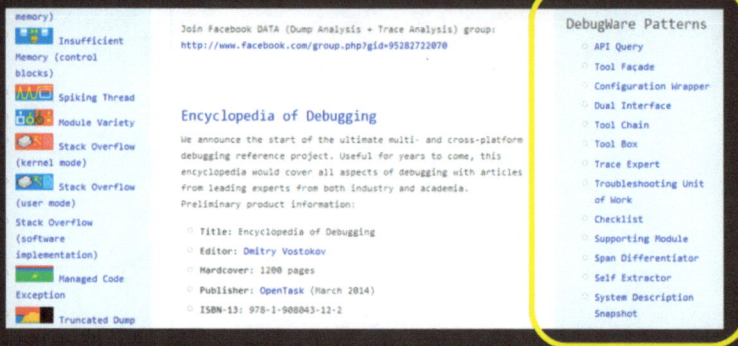

Troubleshooting Unit of Work

http://www.dumpanalysis.org/blog/index.php/2009/09/21/debugware-patterns-part-8/

Patterns

http://www.dumpanalysis.org/blog/index.php/debugware-patterns/

Case study

http://www.dumpanalysis.org/blog/index.php/2009/10/30/debugware-patterns-a-case-study-part-1/

Now we provide links for Debugware patterns. There not so many of them now but more will be coming in the future. One example is **TUW**, **T**roubleshooting **U**nit of **W**ork, where a certain troubleshooting action or a set of actions is factored out into a separate module. If you visit Dump Analysis Portal and scroll its main page you would see Debugware patterns on the right hand side after the trace analysis pattern list.

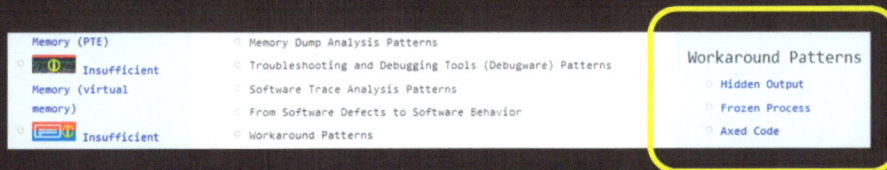

Frozen Process
http://www.dumpanalysis.org/blog/index.php/2010/01/25/workaround-patterns-part-2/

Patterns
http://www.dumpanalysis.org/blog/index.php/workaround-patterns/

Not all post-construction problems are amenable to fixes, especially if there are time and resource constraints. In such cases we can use Workaround patterns to provide temporary solutions. For example, **Axing Code** instead of modifying a specific line or freezing a process or removing conflicting applications. There is much work here to expand the pattern list.

Unified Debugging

⊙ Systematic Pattern Language
⊙ Example:

Analysis Patterns	*Shared Buffer Overwrite*
Architectural Patterns	*Debug Event Subscription / Notification*
Design Patterns	*Punctuated Execution*
Implementation Patterns	*Breakpoint (software and hardware)*
Usage Patterns	*Kernel vs. user space breakpoints*

© 2011 Memory Dump Analysis Services

Shared Buffer Overwrite

http://www.dumpanalysis.org/blog/index.php/2010/10/18/crash-dump-analysis-patterns-part-110/

We also started the unification of software behavior analysis patterns with debugging architecture, design, implementation and usage. This is analogous to software construction where a problem analysis leads to various software engineering phases. The important difference here is the addition of debugging usage patterns, for example, kernel vs. user space breakpoints. To differentiate this systematic approach from the various published ad hoc debugging patterns we call it **Unified Debugging Pattern Language**. Architecture, design, and implementation parts can also correspond to various Debugware patterns.

The last section is about future directions (what to expect in the nearest future).

Structural Memory Patterns

- Examples: Memory Region and Region Boundary
- DumpAnalysis.org

OMAP Code Optimization

No Component Symbols

Insufficient Memory (committed memory)

Insufficient Memory (handle leak)

Insufficient Memory (kernel pool)

Insufficient

Structural Memory Patterns
- Memory Snapshot (Structured or BLOB)
- Aggregate Snapshot
- Snapshot Collection
- Memory Region (Open or Closed)
- Region Boundary
- Memory Hierarchy (General)
- Anchor Region

© 2011 Memory Dump Analysis Services

Memory Region

http://www.dumpanalysis.org/blog/index.php/2010/10/01/structural-memory-patterns-part-4/

Region Boundary

http://www.dumpanalysis.org/blog/index.php/2010/10/01/structural-memory-patterns-part-5/

We can divide memory and trace analysis patterns mostly seen as abnormal software behavior into behavioral and structural catalogues. The goal is to account for normal system-independent structural entities and relationships visible in memory like modules, threads, processes, etc. For example, one such pattern (and also a super-pattern) is called **Memory Snapshot**. It is further subdivided into **Structured Memory Snapshot** and **BLOB Memory Snapshot.** Structured sub-pattern includes:

- Contiguous memory dump files with artificially generated headers (for example, physical or process virtual space memory dump)
- Software trace messages with imposed internal structure

BLOB sub-pattern variety includes address range snapshots without any externally imposed structure, for example, saved by *.writemem* WinDbg command or *ReadProcessMemory* Win32 API and contiguous buffer and raw memory dumps saved by various memory acquisition tools.

Behavioral patterns that relate to Memory Snapshot pattern are:

False Positive Dump

http://www.dumpanalysis.org/blog/index.php/2006/11/01/crash-dump-analysis-patterns-part-3/

Lateral Damage

http://www.dumpanalysis.org/blog/index.php/2006/11/03/crash-dump-analysis-patterns-part-4/

Inconsistent Dump

http://www.dumpanalysis.org/blog/index.php/2007/01/24/crash-dump-analysis-patterns-part-7/

Truncated Dump

http://www.dumpanalysis.org/blog/index.php/2007/07/20/crash-dump-analysis-patterns-part-18/

Early Crash Dump

http://www.dumpanalysis.org/blog/index.php/2007/11/21/crash-dump-analysis-patterns-part-37/

Manual Dump (kernel)

http://www.dumpanalysis.org/blog/index.php/2007/12/12/crash-dump-analysis-patterns-part-41a/

Manual Dump (process)

http://www.dumpanalysis.org/blog/index.php/2007/12/17/crash-dump-analysis-patterns-part-41b/

Corrupt Dump

http://www.dumpanalysis.org/blog/index.php/2008/01/24/crash-dump-analysis-patterns-part-43/

No Process Dumps

http://www.dumpanalysis.org/blog/index.php/2008/01/30/crash-dump-analysis-patterns-part-45/

No System Dumps

http://www.dumpanalysis.org/blog/index.php/2008/01/31/crash-dump-analysis-patterns-part-46/

Self-Dump

http://www.dumpanalysis.org/blog/index.php/2008/02/22/crash-dump-analysis-patterns-part-52/

Abridged Dump

http://www.dumpanalysis.org/blog/index.php/2010/08/04/crash-dump-analysis-patterns-part-104/

Other examples include **Memory Region** and **Region Boundary** such as a stack and its guard page.

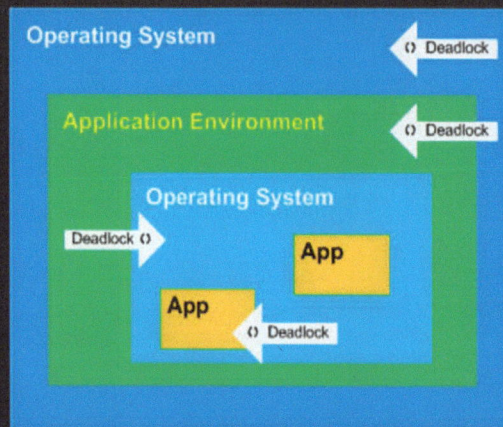

Next I'm working at is the so called domain pattern hierarchy where we have the same repeated patterns through software layers such as virtualization. For example, an OS can have managed or interpreted code environment (such as .NET and Java) with another OS implemented in .NET language and Java (as a research project, for example), the latter OS can have its own Apps written in the same or completely different language. As you can see a deadlock is possible in every layer although pattern internals would be different in each case.

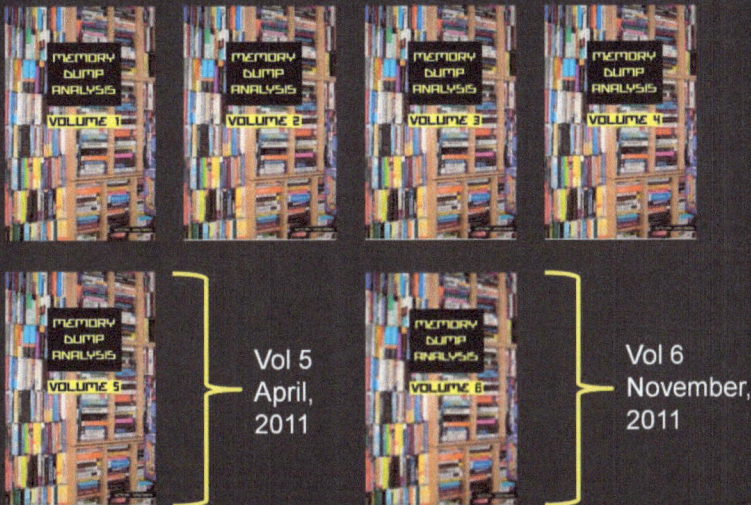

Pattern-Driven Memory Dump Analysis

http://community.citrix.com/blogs/citrite/dmitryv

Memory Dump and Trace Analysis: A Unified Pattern Approach

http://www.debuggingexperts.com/memory-dump-trace-analysis-unified-pattern-approach

Advanced Software Debugging Reference

http://www.forensicanalysis.org/advanced-software-debugging-reference

This slide has links for further study including a presentation with full transcript comments about pattern-driven memory dump analysis I delivered 2 years ago and a full case study from Debugging Experts Magazine.

Note: I was planning to release volume 5 before this presentation but I couldn't. Should be published by the end of this month or in early April. Volume 6 is scheduled by the end of this year.

Software Narratology

Introduction

Version 1.0

Dmitry Vostokov
Memory Dump Analysis Services

Published by OpenTask, Republic of Ireland

OpenTask books and magazines are available through booksellers and distributors worldwide. For further information or comments send requests to press@opentask.com.

A CIP catalogue record for this book is available from the British Library.

ISBN-l3: 978-1-908043-07-8 (Paperback)

First printing, 2012

Software Narratology

Introduction

Version 1.0

Dmitry Vostokov
Memory Dump Analysis Services

Hello Everyone, my name is Dmitry Vostokov and I introduce software narratology today. This is a version one of the Webinar in order not to overwelm you with concepts if you are not familiar with narratology. So I decided to keep this presentation as simple as possible and gradually introduce you to the concepts.

Prerequisites

Ability to read strories

These prerequisites are very simple and I suppose you all enjoy reading stories. The whole new discipline was born because I needed to convince myself to enjoy reading software traces and event logs.

A Story

After a long search a Hero found a castle and tried to open its gate. It's closed. The Hero needed a key.

Let's analyze this story fragment from some fiction: *After a long search a Hero found a castle and tried to open its gate. It's closed. The Hero needed a key.*

A Narrative

A long search

A Hero found a castle

The Hero tried to open the castle gate

The gate was closed

The Hero needed a key

> **Definition:** narrative is a representation of events and state changes.

Let's break the story into the sequence of events:

A long search
A Hero found a castle
The Hero tried to open the castle gate
The gate was closed
The Hero needed a key

From these events we can construct any representation such as the text we read previously or it can be a movie or a graphic.

Definition: Narrative is a representation of events and state changes.

A Software Story

After a long computation a Component ABC tried to save computed results in a file. Access denied. The Component needed to have certain rights.

Now consider this real software story: *After a long computation a Component ABC tried to save computed results in a file. Access denied. The Component needed to have certain rights.* It sounds very similar to the the previous fictional story and you see the Component ABC plays a Hero role. The file is the castle and access right is the key.

A Software Narrative

Time	Component	Message
[...]		
12:11	ABC	Compute: enter
18:11	ABC	Compute: 50%
22:25	ABC	Compute: exit
22:26	ABC	Save to file results.dat: 0x5
[...]		

Definition: Software narrative is a representation of software events and changes of state.

If we break our software story into software-defined events we get a software trace or event log. Where did this narrative come from? Who does create such narratives?

Definition: Software narrative is a representation of software events and changes of state.

Software Construction I

```
Program ABC
begin
    Compute.start()
    do
        completion = Compute.continue()
    while completion <> 100%
    Compute.end()
    result = Save(Compute.results(), "results.dat")
end
```

Software developers add code during software construction phase to generate such event descriptions during software execution to assist themselves and more often other people in problem solving such as software troubleshooting and debugging.

Software Post-construction

```
>   run ABC
>   print results.dat
[empty]
>
```

However, during software post-construction phase a user runs the program and gets an empty file with no results. The user opens a support case and ...

Software Construction II

```
Program ABC
begin
    WriteEvent("Compute: enter")
    Compute.start()
    do
        completion = Compute.continue()
        WriteEvent("Compute: ", completion)
    while completion <> 100%
    Compute.end()
    WriteEvent("Compute: exit")
    result = Save(Compute.results(), "results.dat")
    WriteEvent("Save to file results.dat: ", result)
end
```

... a software engineer modifies code to add events. This could also have been done during the software construction phase in anticipation of possible future software problems. We come back to this anticipation shortly.

A History

- May 7, 2009: First trace analysis pattern

- May 29, 2009: Interview on Tracing Tools

- June 12, 2009: First definition of software narratology

- March 20, 2012: Second definition of software narratology

Now a bit of history. Please note that this is itself a historical narrative, a sequence of events and state of mind changes. Earlier in 2009 I was trying to make sense of software trace analysis. Historically I started with full time memory dump analysis more than 8 years ago. After some time I had to analyze very complex software logs with millions events from dozens of processes, hundreds of components and threads. There was no time to learn millions of source code lines as well. If in memory dumps a problem was always immediately visible to me due to numerous patterns then in software logs it was not. So I started discerning patterns to help me with trace analysis. However I came to pattern-writing block as there were not so many discernible product-independent patterns. During the fateful interview about tracing tools I was asked about how to explain software traces to a general software user. Fortunately, a few weeks before, I started reading books on literary theory and criticism which mentioned the notion of a narrative. So all this came to my mind and I explained software tracing as stories of computation. After that I came up with the first definition of software narratology as an application of narratology to software traces and logs. All subsequent product-independent trace analysis patterns (almost 50 of them) were discerned using this narratological perspective. During the next 2 years I was reading a lot on literature and recently came up with an idea to extend software narratology to the whole domain of software including software construction phases.

May 7, 2009

First trace analysis pattern:

http://www.dumpanalysis.org/blog/index.php/2009/04/28/trace-analysis-patterns-part-1/

May 29, 2009

Interview on Tracing Tools:

http://support.citrix.com/article/ctx121366

June 12, 2009

First definition of software narratology:

http://www.dumpanalysis.org/blog/index.php/2009/06/12/software-narratology-a-definition/

March 20, 2012

Second definition of software narratology:

http://www.dumpanalysis.org/blog/index.php/2012/03/20/what-is-a-software-narrative/

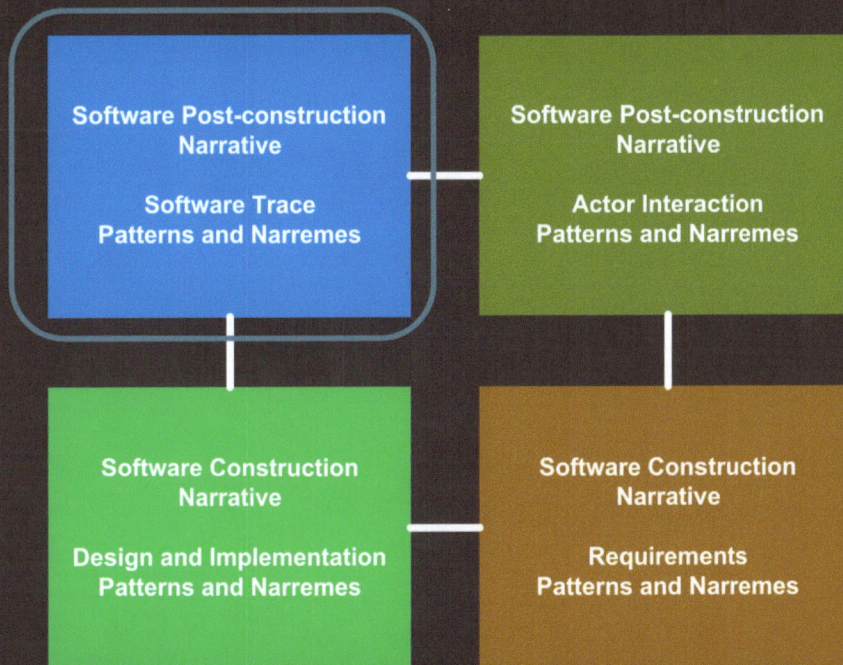

An SN Square

| Software Post-construction Narrative — Software Trace Patterns and Narremes | Software Post-construction Narrative — Actor Interaction Patterns and Narremes |
| Software Construction Narrative — Design and Implementation Patterns and Narremes | Software Construction Narrative — Requirements Patterns and Narremes |

© 2012 Memory Dump Analysis Services

This is a software narratological square where the top row deals wth software post-construction phase and the bottom row deals with software construction phase. The left column deals with software implementation aspects and the right column deals with requirements and use cases. In this introduction we only discuss the top left square related to post-construction software stories: relevant to software users and technical support and maintenance personnel. Other squares will be discussed in subsequent expanded versions of this introduction. The concept of a software narreme will be introduced shortly.

Story, Plot, Representation

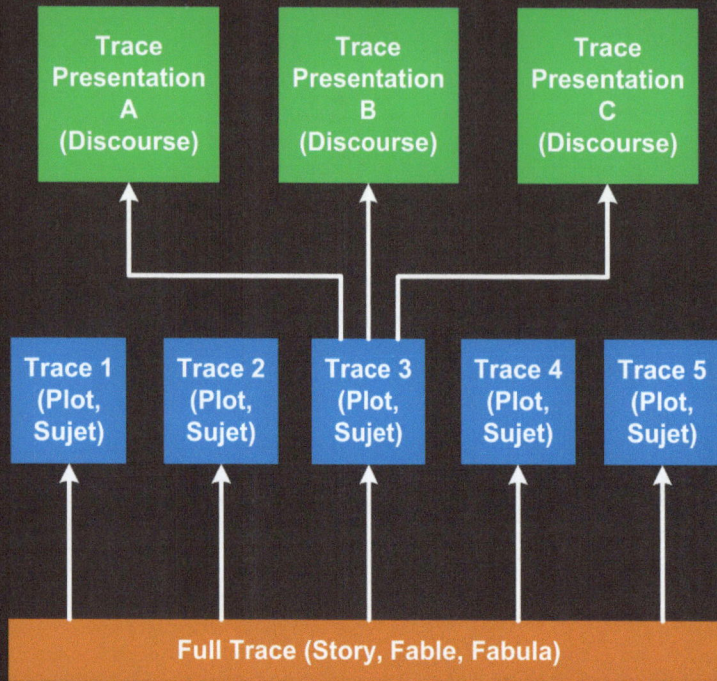

Now we briefly discuss yet another aspect of narrative: its representation. The events of the whole full story (also called fable or fabula) can be rearranged in numerous ways to create various plots also called sujets (for example, with suspention as in fiction thrillers). Before or during software execution the generation of certain event categories can be switched off or on. When engineers analyze software traces they hide certain events in order to reduce the size of a trace. So we get different software plots or sujects from the possible full software story or fabula. But every individual plot can be presented differently, for example, in a novel or a poem, and even in a movie. The same goes for software stories as well.

Paratext

- ⊙ Story Text

+

- ⊙ Book cover
- ⊙ Front matter
- ⊙ Back matter

Additional useful concept from narratology is the concept of a paratext. This is additional information about a text useful for its interpretation such as a book cover, an introduction from an editor, notes or the list of other referenced texts.

Front and back matter:
http://en.wikipedia.org/wiki/Book_design

Extended Software Trace

⊙ Software Trace

+

⊙ Supporting Information (pictures, videos, accounts of scenarios and past problem histories, user interviews)

This leads to the concept of an extended software trace that includes supporting information such as pictures, videos, accounts of scenarios and past problem histories, user interviews: all what is necessary to understand a software incident and lead to a problem resolution.

A Software Narreme

- Basic unit of a software narrative

- Examples:

Enter / Exit

Request / Reply

Now we come to a basic unit of software narratives: a software narreme. Here we don't consider a syntactical unit such as an event. Such basic units need to have a semantic aspect as well if they are of any use. We are in the process of their identification and some examples incude **enter / exit** and **request / reply**.

Software Narreme Types

State

Action

Commentary

© 2012 Memory Dump Analysis Services

There are 3 basic software narreme types: **state** and **action** reports and a **commentary**.

SN ⟺ N

- Software Narratology helps Fiction Writers
- Writing and Validation of Historical Narratives

We have already seen that the sudy of fiction helps with structuring and understanding of software stories. So is the other way around and software narratology and its patterns help with understanding fiction and other types of narrative such as historical narratives. Moreover, it can help with fiction writing. If you like science fiction then you are probably familiar with the novel of Philip K. Dick "The Man in the High Castle". It is a known fact that the author used a fiction creating device, an ancient Chinese book **I Ching** (pronounces /ˌiː ˈtʃɪŋ/), to guide story construction. We can also use various software traces to create story and plot fragments. We just need to replace components, processes and threads with various agents and institutions.

Software Narratology helps Fiction Writers:
http://www.dumpanalysis.org/blog/index.php/2012/02/13/software-narratology-helps-fiction-writers/

Writing and Validation of Historical Narratives:
http://www.dumpanalysis.org/blog/index.php/2012/03/11/writing-and-validation-of-historical-narratives-part-1/

Software Narrative Genres

Definition: Ways of presenting software narrative.

Different platforms and products use different formats for software logs and traces.

Definition: Software narrative genre is a way of presenting software narratives.

Narrative Isomorphism

Definition: Correspondence in narrative structure.

Software narratology strives to discern what is common to all software stories. For example, so far we have identified almost 50 patterns.

Definition: Narrative isomorphism is a correspondence in narrative structure.

Computer Diagnostics Now

Vendor A:

Has its own proprietary event logging formats and its own diagnostics and analysis tools

Vendor B:

Has its own proprietary event logging formats and its own different diagnostics and analysis tools

Software diagnostics now is fragmented across products, technologies, and vendors. Different products have different diagnostic report formats. Even when a certain diagnostics technology is used by different software vendors such as Event Tracing for Windows reporting formats and styles differ greatly and in ad hoc manner. A unified approach is needed that doesn't mandate rules but takes into account the diverse nature of computer diagnostics. We believe Software Narratology is such an approach.

Benefits of sofware narratological approach include anticipatory software construction and product independent software problem solving, where we use the term "anticipatory" in the sense of annotation your code with software events in such a way as to help with software trace analysis later. Product independence uses narrative isomorphism, genre aspects, software trace narremes and patterns to analyze software traces and logs in the similar way regardless of software platforms, technologies, products and vendors.

Anticipatory Software

Definition: Anticipates post-construction problem analysis.

By looking at software traces as narrative stories a software engineer would better anticipate the needs of software maintainers and technical support and escalation engineers by constructing better event descriptions.

Definition: Anticipatory software construction anticipates post-construction problem analysis.

Software narratological perspective gives a unified framework of patterns to look for when analyzing software traces and logs from diverse products, platforms and technologies. Knowledge of trace analysis patterns lowers a learning curve during transition to maintainance and support of a different product. In tiered support organizations it provides a unified pattern language to report and discuss diagnostic reports and alerts, problem incidents and their artifacts.

Software Narratrive Patterns:

http://www.dumpanalysis.org/blog/index.php/trace-analysis-patterns/

Further Reading

Narratology

- An Introduction to Narratology (by Monika Fludernik)
- The Cambridge Introduction to Narrative (by H. Porter Abbott)

Software Narratology

- Pattern Catalog
- SoftwareNarratology.com
- Memory Dump Analysis Anthology: Volumes 3, 4, 5, 6, 7, ...
- Software Trace and Memory Dump Analysis: Patterns, Tools, Processes and Best Practices

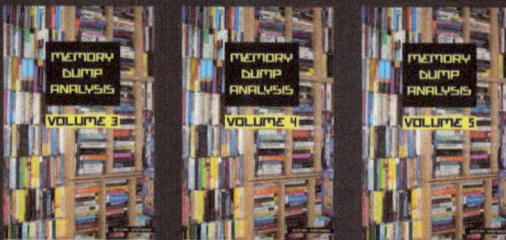

Volume 6 is in preparation (April-May, 2012)
Volume 7 is planned for the end of 2012

There are two basic introductions to narrative that I found useful. I also include links to the emerging discipline of Software Narratology. Some edited articles started to appear in Volume 3 of Memory Dump Analysis Anthology.

www.SoftwareNarratology.com
Now points to www.DumpAnalysis.org and www.TraceAnalysis.org

Pattern Catalog:
http://www.dumpanalysis.org/blog/index.php/trace-analysis-patterns/

Memory Dump Analysis Anthology:
http://www.dumpanalysis.com/ultimate-memory-analysis-reference

Software Trace and Memory Dump Analysis: Patterns, Tools, Processes and Best Practices:
http://www.dumpanalysis.com/STMDA-materials

Pattern-Driven
Software Diagnostics
Introduction

Version 1.0

Dmitry Vostokov
Software Diagnostics Services

Published by OpenTask, Republic of Ireland

OpenTask books and magazines are available through booksellers and distributors worldwide. For further information or comments send requests to press@opentask.com.

A CIP catalogue record for this book is available from the British Library.

ISBN-l3: 978-1-908043-38-2 (Paperback)

First printing, 2013

Hello Everyone, my name is Dmitry Vostokov and I introduce pattern-driven software diagnostics today. This is a version one of the Webinar in order not to overwelm you with concepts. I decided to keep this presentation as simple as possible and as short as possible.

Prerequisites

Interest in **software** diagnostics

These prerequisites are very simple and I suppose you all enjoy diagnosing software problems and not only software because there are many similarities with other disciplines such as medicine, hardware, and aircraft maintenance.

Why?

- No comprehensive systematic study of software diagnostics

- Ad hoc services

- Traditionally associated with troubleshooting and debugging

Why there is such a Webinar at all? After doing memory dump and software trace professionally full time for nearly 9 years I realized that what I was doing is called software diagnostics. At the same time I wasn't able to find any comprehensive and systematic study of it and it looks like every software vendor provides its own vision of it, uses its own language and tools. Perhaps, it is the fact that software diagnostics was traditionally associated with troubleshooting and debugging masked its importance as a separate discipline.

© 2012 Software Diagnostics Services

It was beneficial for me to read about medical diagnostics as there are many similarities there and find out that today we share the same goals that were outlined in a book "Diagnosis: Philosophical and Medical Perspectives" 20-30 years ago when medical diagnostics went through a computer revolution. Our goals are to outline a comprehensive methodology including processes and common language and understand technological limits and at the same time see what services are needed.

Diagnostics

- Based on pattern recognition:
  symptoms and signs

- Systems approach

Here in this Webinar we mainly provide parallels with medical diagnostics that we call just diagnostics for short. Traditionally diagnostics is based on two pillars: pattern recognition through symptoms and signs and systems approach: a set of interrelated parts having structure and functions.

Software Diagnostics

- Based on pattern recognition: *symptoms and signs*

- Systems approach

Software diagnostics is based on the same principle. In this Webinar we are concerned only with the first part: pattern recognition, A systemic perspective and systems thinking will be covered in the second Webinar (also published as a book, ISBN-13 978-1-908043-39-9). At the end I put a slide with information on how to register there.

.

Symptoms

- ⊙ **User or system complaints**

  Error message
  Slow system
  High CPU usage

- ⊙ **Histories**

Symptoms include user or system complaints. It is necessary to include software symptoms such as error message boxes. And like in diagnostics we have histories of complains which can also be considered as patterns of software description.

Signs

Traditional artifact patterns

- ⊙ Situation dependent: *memory or handle leak*

- ⊙ Specific vs. non-specific: *spike, leak vs. access violation*

Signs are what traditionally were called patterns in artifacts such as live memory and postmortem dumps and software traces and logs. Such signs are situation dependent: what in one case can be considered a leak such as 5,000 handles might be quite normal for another case. Also some signs are specific and lead to easy shallow diagnosis such as CPU spike and some signs are non-specific and require a deeper analysis such as access violation.

Pattern Groupings

Syndromes

- [Pattern Interaction](#)

- [Pattern Succession](#)

In diagnostics a group of associated symptoms and signs is called a syndrome. Software diagnostics distinguishes pattern groups as pattern interaction and pattern succession. The former one covers repeated cases where patterns occur together without any visible causal links and the latter deals with sets of patterns that have causal links. Looking at pattern interaction cases it is easy to see that some patterns precede others, for example, heap corruption caused by an error message box and therefore blocks other threads, creating conditions for another pattern to appear, wait chains. Blocked threads may block other coupled processes creating inter-process wait chains and finally inter-machine wait chains. Some patterns are most likely found in succession and other patterns are less likely effect abnormal conditions. Such pattern sequences can help in troubleshooting, debugging and root cause analysis.

Pattern Interaction:
http://www.dumpanalysis.org/blog/index.php/pattern-cooperation/

Pattern Succession:
http://www.dumpanalysis.org/blog/index.php/2010/06/03/succession-of-patterns-part-2/

Problem Solving

- Diagnosis ➡ treatment

- **Software Diagnosis** ➡ problem resolution

Diagnostics is separate from treatment although post-treatment monitoring also considered as diagnostics. The same should be for software diagnostics: it is separate from post-construction problem resolution activities such as troubleshooting and debugging. Performance monitoring is a part of software diagnostics proper.

Problem Solving

- **Workaround Patterns**

- **Unified Debugging Patterns**

Treatment or problem solving and resolution phase has its own patterns such as workaround and unified debugging. For further discussion here please see a reference to pattern-driven software problem solving presentation at the end of this Webinar.

Workaround Patterns:
http://www.dumpanalysis.org/blog/index.php/workaround-patterns/

Unified Debugging Patterns:
http://www.dumpanalysis.org/blog/index.php/workaround-patterns/

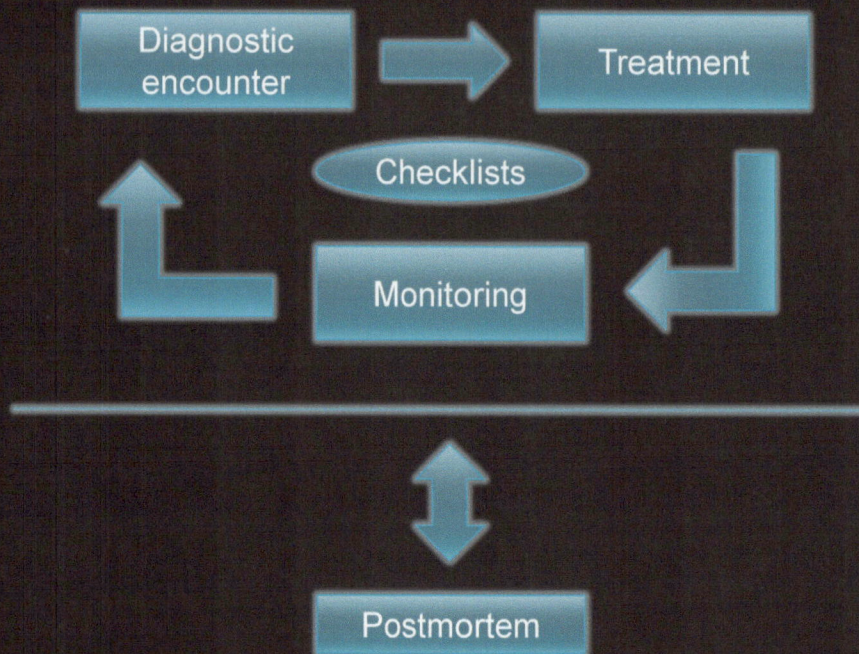

I'd like to say a few words about a diagnostics process. It should be iterative based on checklists and include postmortem analysis of past diagnostic encounters in the light of success of failure of subsequent treatment and monitoring as diagnostics tests.

Now we briefly cover checklists. They should be artifact based such as, for example, checklists for memory dump and software trace analysis. Of course, there are some common checks so they should be factored into a more general level. This leads to layered checklists.

Memory Dump Analysis:
http://www.dumpanalysis.org/blog/index.php/2007/06/20/crash-dump-analysis-checklist/

Software Trace Analysis:
http://www.dumpanalysis.org/blog/index.php/2011/03/10/software-trace-analysis-checklist/

Artifact Baselines

- Memory Dumps: Reference Stack Traces

- Software Logs: Master Traces

© 2012 Software Diagnostics Services

Software diagnostics is useless if we don't have established NULL cases: cases where the behavior is expected. Here master traces and reference stack traces is of great help.

Memory Dumps: Reference Stack Traces

http://www.dumpanalysis.org/blog/index.php/reference-stack-traces/

Software Logs: Master Traces

http://www.dumpanalysis.org/blog/index.php/2011/01/30/trace-analysis-patterns-part-36/

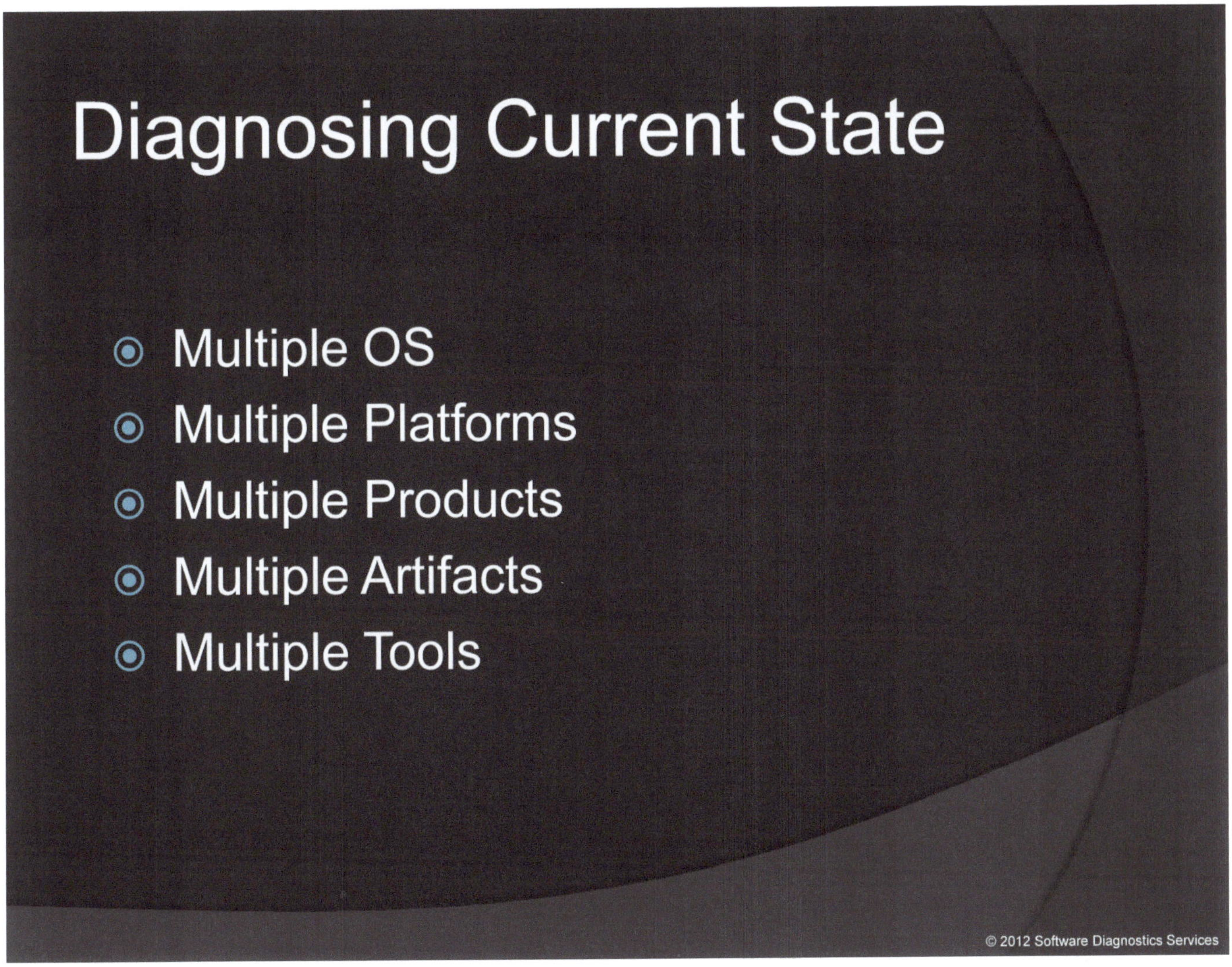

Diagnosing Current State

- ⊙ Multiple OS
- ⊙ Multiple Platforms
- ⊙ Multiple Products
- ⊙ Multiple Artifacts
- ⊙ Multiple Tools

The current state of software diagnostics is abnormal as well: multiplicity of everything without anything unifying.

Pattern Language

- ◉ Structural and behavioural patterns

(S,B)-systems

- ◉ Antipatterns

Example: Inquisitor

- ◉ Pattern Explanations

Unified software diagnostics pattern language is the cure for the current diagnostics illness. Antipatterns are also of help here. Inquisitor antipattern, for example, describes an engineer who only demands more and more data without giving any explanation why it is needed. Software Diagnostics Institute will also provide ready-to-use less technical explanations for specific patterns.

Pattern Catalog

⊙ Problem Description Analysis

⊙ UI Problem Analysis

⊙ Memory Dump Analysis

⊙ Software Trace Analysis

Here are links to pattern catalogs in their current states. The first two links cover symptoms and the next two links – signs in memory dumps and software traces.

Problem Description Analysis:
http://www.dumpanalysis.org/blog/index.php/2012/03/11/software-problem-description-patterns-part-1/

UI Problem Analysis:
http://www.dumpanalysis.org/blog/index.php/2011/07/14/user-interface-problem-analysis-patterns-part-1/

Memory Dump Analysis:
http://www.dumpanalysis.org/blog/index.php/crash-dump-analysis-patterns/

Software Trace Analysis:
http://www.dumpanalysis.org/blog/index.php/trace-analysis-patterns/

© 2012 Software Diagnostics Services

There is also a need to have patterns for software diagnostics itself independent from specific artifact analysis patterns. Examples of such meta-patterns include First Fault, Multiple Patterns, NULL case (healthy system), NULL Diagnosis (nothing found) and requires Second Opinion, Noise that needs to be filtered or paid attention to as it might hide further patterns of interest.

First Fault:

http://www.dumpanalysis.org/blog/index.php/2012/06/09/patterns-of-software-diagnostics-part-1/

One of the benefits of pattern language for software diagnostics is its uniform description of the same behavioral problems in different systems and even discovery of new possible patterns previously going undetected or not paid enough attention to. Here I provide links for 2 examples: multiple exceptions pattern when several threads experience exceptions independently when running on multiple CPUs and spiking thread pattern.

Multiple Exceptions (Windows):
http://www.dumpanalysis.org/blog/index.php/2010/05/16/models-for-memory-and-trace-analysis-patterns-part-1/

Multiple Exceptions (Mac OS X):
http://www.dumpanalysis.org/blog/index.php/2012/04/04/crash-dump-analysis-patterns-part-1-mac-os-x/

Spiking Thread (Windows):
http://www.dumpanalysis.org/blog/index.php/2007/05/11/crash-dump-analysis-patterns-part-14/

Spiking Thread (Mac OS X):
http://www.dumpanalysis.org/blog/index.php/2012/05/09/crash-dump-analysis-patterns-part-14-mac-os-x/

Performance Monitoring

Trace Patterns:

- ⊙ <u>Counter Value</u>
- ⊙ Global Monotonicity
- ⊙ Constant Value

© 2012 Software Diagnostics Services

Performance monitoring is a part of software diagnostics and the same patterns can be used there, for example, **Counter Value** pattern. A counter value is some variable in memory, for example, a module variable, that is updated periodically to reflect some aspect of state or it can be calculated from different such variables and presented in trace messages. Therefore, all other trace analysis patterns such as **Adjoint Thread** (can be visualized via different colors on a graph), **Focus of Tracing**, **Characteristic Message Block** (for graphs), **Activity Region**, **Significant Event**, and others can be applicable here. There are also some specific patterns such as **Global Monotonicity** and **Constant Value** that we publish later on. Global monotonicity is a case when performance for shorter period fluctuates around increasing average value. Constant counter values can be signs for a process freeze and wait chains.

Counter Value:
http://www.dumpanalysis.org/blog/index.php/2012/06/23/trace-analysis-patterns-part-51/

Monitoring Best Practices

Example: artifact collection

Software Tracing Best Practices

One example of best practices to follow is an artifact collection. This includes providing supporting and context information that helps finding anchor messages in large software traces.

Software Tracing Best Practices:
http://www.dumpanalysis.org/blog/index.php/2010/12/29/software-tracing-best-practices-part-1/

One of the current goals of Software Diagnostics Institute (www.DumpAnalysis.org) is to develop a range of software diagnostics certifications so that individuals can demonstrate knowledge of pattern-driven software diagnostics for troubleshooting and debugging purposes such as memory dump and software trace analysis and the ability to use uniform methodology and pattern language for different OS and debuggers, for example, to use the same language for analysis of software logs created by different tracing tools. Another advantage is using the same language across different teams and even departments and even help with hiring right people with the right skills. Uniform pattern language also eliminates steep learning curves when supporting different products and vendors. Another goal is corporate enterprise maturity certification. Some companies do not use any methodology and don't have any processes for software diagnostics and even if they do they use different languages to communicate their analysis of software artifacts to other companies when doing software troubleshooting and debugging in complex environments that include software from different vendors. Such certification for post-construction phase complements software construction certifications such as Capability Maturity Model.

Memory Dump Analysis:
http://www.dumpanalysis.com/memory-dump-analysis-certification-outline

Software Diagnostics Maturity:
http://www.dumpanalysis.com/software-diagnostics-maturity

Diagnostics Audit

Catalog of Diagnostic Errors

Audit Service from MDAS

- ⊙ Checklists for checklists
- ⊙ Diagnostics for diagnostics

A few words about a diagnostics audit. It is always possible to have a second opinion especially for complex software incidents so one of goals is to create a catalog of diagnostics errors to avoid common errors. It is also good to have checklists for checklists to update the latter regularly and use diagnostics for diagnostics from time to time to improve the whole service. One such service is an audit service from the former Memory Dump Analysis Services (now Software Diagnostics Services).

Audit Service:
http://www.dumpanalysis.com/memory-dump-analysis-audit-service

Now I'd like to say a few words about the human side of software diagnostics. In cases of great diagnostic load for engineers they obviously become tired and that reduces their efficiency and also affects their ability to provide more deep diagnostics because what happens sometimes (and this is a pattern of software diagnostics as well) is that when an engineer sees one pattern then the whole process is stopped but if diagnostics is done a bit deeper some other patterns may be found.

Is Automation Possible?

- Growth of data
- Growth of complexity

- Impossibility of complete automation
- Only computer-assisted diagnostics

And then there is a question because of that human side: is automation possible for software diagnostics? We think that it is impossible to provide a complete automation because of constant growth of data and growth of complexity, and the only alternative is to use computer-assisted diagnostics for humans, that a partial automation is only possible.

Systems and Diagnostics

General Software Diagnostics Theory

Introduction to Systemic Software Diagnostics

As I mentioned at the start, in addition to pattern recognition systemic perspective is of great help in software diagnostics (as in medical diagnostics). The whole journey for me started almost 6 years ago when I realized that systems theory helps in memory dump analysis. Please refer to a second Webinar on software diagnostics from this perspective (also published as a book, ISBN-13 978-1-908043-39-9).

Malware Analysis

Malware + Victimware

Victimware: The Missing Part of the Equation

Software diagnostics can naturally be extended to malware and victimware analysis where the latter includes innocent victims of malware, victims of other coding mistakes or deliberate subversion and some start as a part of crimeware and malware but eventually become victims themselves through coding mistakes (also published as a book, ISBN-13 978-1-908043-50-4).

Further Reading

Diagnostics

- Diagnosis: Philosophical and Medical Perspectives (by Agassi & Laor)

Software Diagnostics

- Software Diagnostics Institute
- Memory Dump Analysis Anthology: Volumes 1, 2, 3, 4, 5, 6, 7, …
  Volume 6 is in preparation (June, 2012)
  Volume 7 is planned for the end of 2012
- Software Trace and Memory Dump Analysis: Patterns, Tools, Processes and Best Practices
- Introduction to Pattern-Driven Software Problem Solving
- Cloud Memory Dump Analysis
- Fundamentals of Complete Crash and Hang Memory Dump Analysis
- Introduction to Software Narratology

There is one useful book on medical diagnostics that I found useful and already mentioned it. I also included links to relevant presentations and books.

Software Diagnostics Institute:

http://www.dumpanalysis.org

Memory Dump Analysis Anthology:

http://www.dumpanalysis.com/ ultimate-memory-analysis-reference

Software Trace and Memory Dump Analysis: Patterns, Tools, Processes and Best Practices:

http://www.dumpanalysis.com/STMDA-materials

Introduction to Pattern-Driven Software Problem Solving:

http://www.dumpanalysis.com/PDSPSI-materials

Cloud Memory Dump Analysis:

http://www.dumpanalysis.com/CMDA-materials

Fundamentals of Complete Crash and Hang Memory Dump Analysis:

http://www.dumpanalysis.com/FCMDA-materials-Rev2

Introduction to Software Narratology:

http://www.dumpanalysis.com/Introduction-Software-Narratology-materials

Systemic
Software Diagnostics
Introduction

Version 1.0

Dmitry Vostokov
Software Diagnostics Services

Published by OpenTask, Republic of Ireland

OpenTask books and magazines are available through booksellers and distributors worldwide. For further information or comments send requests to press@opentask.com.

A CIP catalogue record for this book is available from the British Library.

ISBN-l3: 978-1-908043-39-9 (Paperback)

First printing, 2013

Hello Everyone, my name is Dmitry Vostokov and I introduce systemic software diagnostics today. This is a version one of the Webinar in order not to overwelm you with concepts. I decided to keep this presentation as simple as possible and as short as possible.

Prerequisites

Interest in software diagnostics and
in general systems theory

I suppose you all enjoy diagnosing software problems but feel a bit restricted by the traditional software troubleshooting and debugging techniques. If you are also bored to death by software trace analysis in a large software factory you may find a material presented here refreshing. But first we need to explain some phrases we use such as software diagnostics and also systems theory that is sometimes called general systems theory.

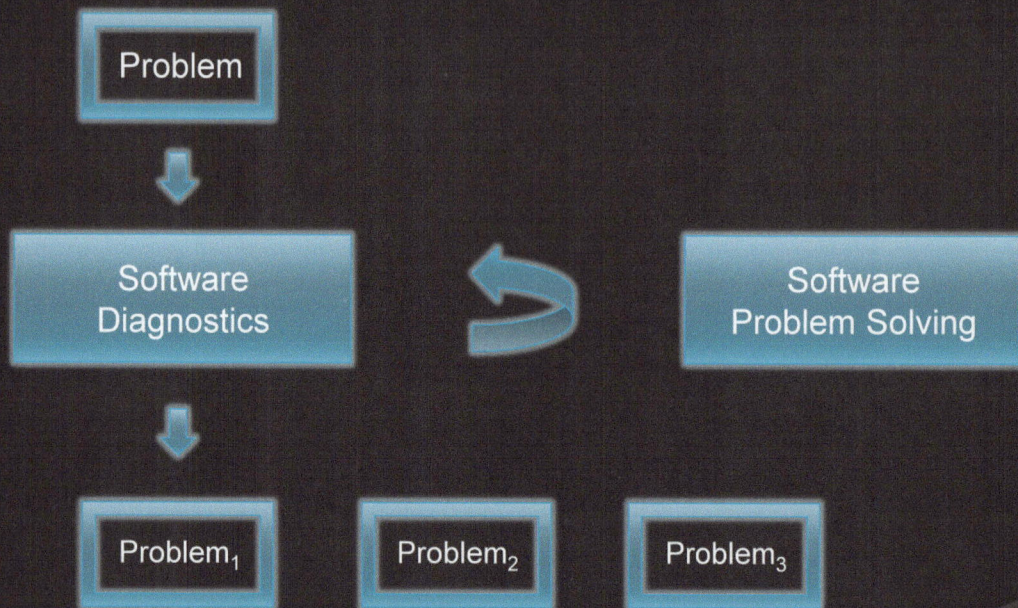

Software Diagnostics can be defined as recognition of patterns of abnormal (or irregular) software structure and behavior in various software artifacts such as memory snapshots and software traces and logs. It needs to be distinct from software problem solving because there can be unnoticed, hidden problems that first need to be diagnosed. This is especially true for system monitoring and diagnosing emergent problems. At the same time software diagnostics is a part of software problem solving such as software troubleshooting and debugging that is always done incrementally and iteratively.

5

General Systems-Theory

Now we try to give a definition to systems theory with a focus on software systems. Please find that we stress on generality of systems theories not a theory of general systems here as there is no such thing as a general system. Thanks to **Facets of Systems Science** book that pointed to that distinction. I put a reference to such a wonderful book at the end of this presentation. A diagram here makes the notion of systems clear. An exampe such as a buiding is too trivial to discuss here. For, a non-trivial example, we can find a narrative fiction system in a real or imaginary world as clearly embedded and delineated with certain narrative parts serving various functions. At the same time consider a bounded region of memory with components inside associated with certain functions and having interfaces. So we are concerned with general similarities in organized systems and not with banalities such as statements that a software system consists of subsystems.

Why?

- Organized Complexity of Software

- Software as Human Artifact

- Problem Solving

Why do we need general systems approach? Because of organized complexity of software as human artefacts we would like to look at other organized complex artefacts of human activity and find common traits to improve our diagnostics and ultimately problem solving ability.

Goals

- ⊚ Ideas from General Systems-Theory

- ⊚ Applications to Software Diagnostics

This Webinar is a loose association of ideas from general systems theory with proposed and already implemented applications to diagnostics, troubleshooting and debugging. Due to time constraints I didn't include all that I planned initially with many slides omitted so I plan to update this webinar next year or include missing material in other webinars.

Software diagnostics can be defined as a search for patterns in software execution artifacts so it is essentially pattern-driven. This aspect was covered in the previous Webinar on pattern-driven software diagnostics and a link to it you can find at the end of this presentation on Resources slide. Here we cover systemic approach: using other systems because of similarities between them and software systems.

System and Environment

- Not My Version

- Changed Environment

- Hooksware

For this obvious statement about the relationship of a software program as a system and its environment I'd like to highlight two patterns such as **Not My Version** (that also exists in a hardware variant) and **Changed Environment** that we discerned some time ago. The recent proliferation of value added software and malware is covered in structural and behavioral patterns related to **Hooksware**.

Not My Version:
http://www.dumpanalysis.org/blog/index.php/2008/06/19/crash-dump-analysis-patterns-part-65/

Changed Environment:
http://www.dumpanalysis.org/blog/index.php/2007/03/19/crash-dump-analysis-patterns-part-10/

Hooksware:
http://www.dumpanalysis.org/blog/index.php/2008/08/10/hooksware/

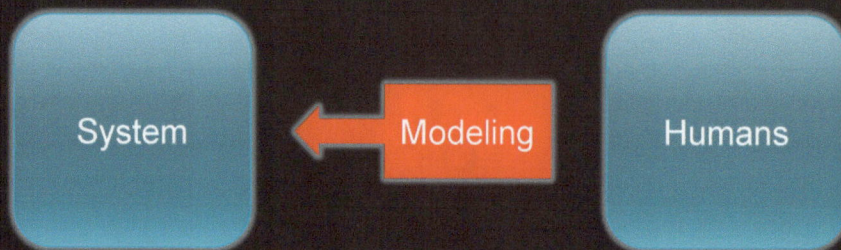

Using Humanities (Past)

System ← Modeling ← Humans

Now we come to the use of common aspects of human systems in software diagnostics that is currently considered as a deterministic mechanistic machine-like system in the mainstream of software engineering and computer science. In the past such anthropomorphic attempts had failed (for example, the so called organismic approaches at the end of the 19th and beginning of 20th century). This was mainly to the unknown functioning of organisms and self-organized societies).

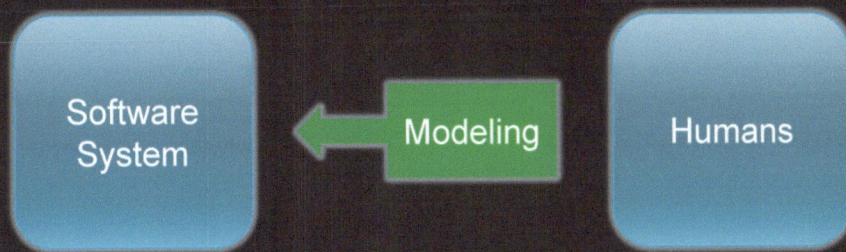

As software systems are created by humans we can use methods of certain disciplines to study software artifacts. Now we know much more in humanities and social sciences compared with a century ago.

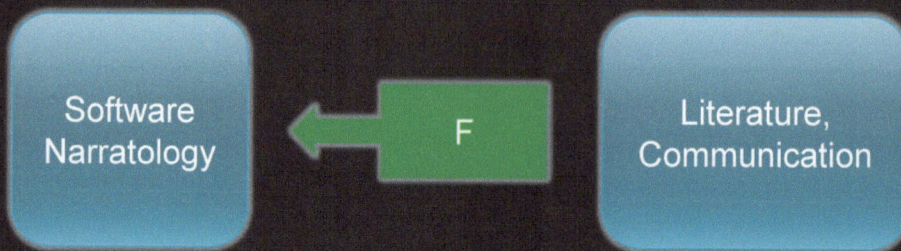

Using Humanities (Example)

Software Narratology ← F ← Literature, Communication

© 2012 Software Diagnostics Services

Typical example is using literary narratology for structuring software traces and logs which are viewed as stories of computation. The link to another webinar on Software Narratology is provided on the resources slide.

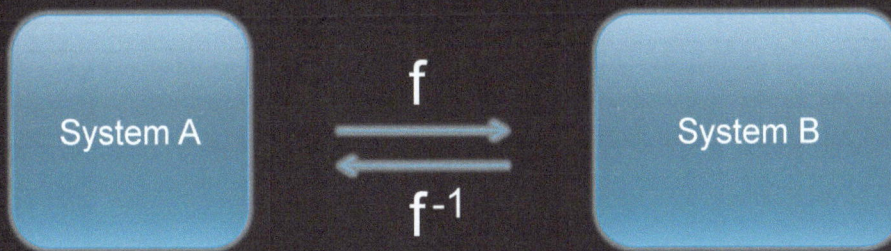

So far we have seen examples of the so called isomorphic systems: systems which have similar properties and methods. This is a typical example of **General Systems Approach**.

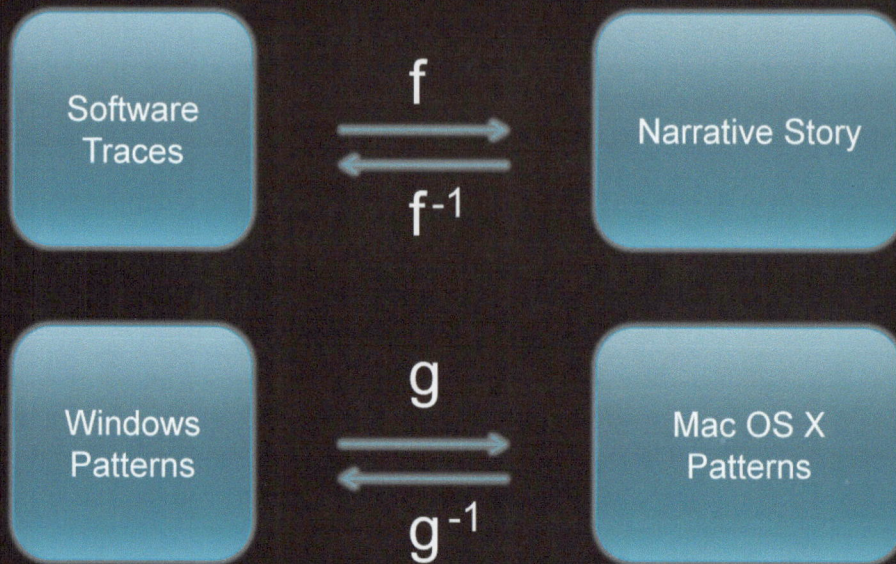

As a consequence we also have isomorphic patterns. For example, patterns of narrative in fiction and in software artifacts. Another example is similarity of memory dump analysis patterns in crash dumps from Windows and core dumps from UNIX-based operating systems.

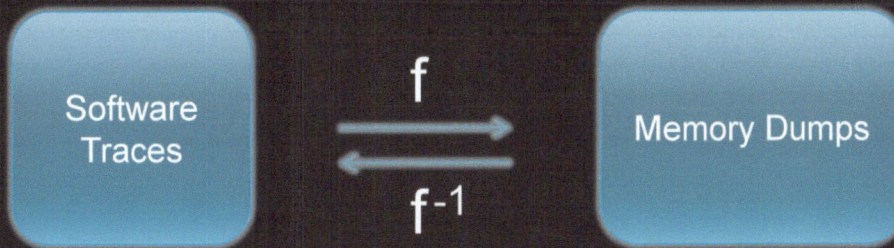

We can also consider similarities between different software artifact types. For example, memory dumps can contain traces and logs can contain minidumps.

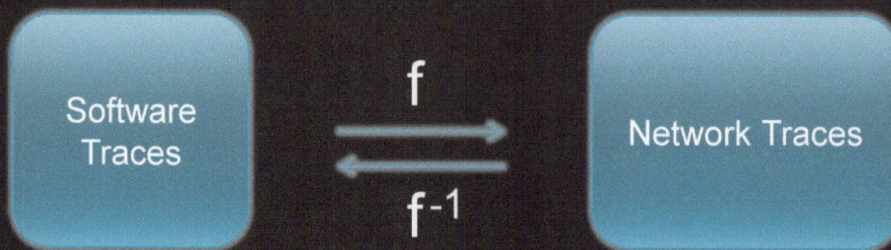

Still another example is similarity between different types of diagnostics activity such as between software trace analysis and network trace analysis where packet headers represent software trace messages.

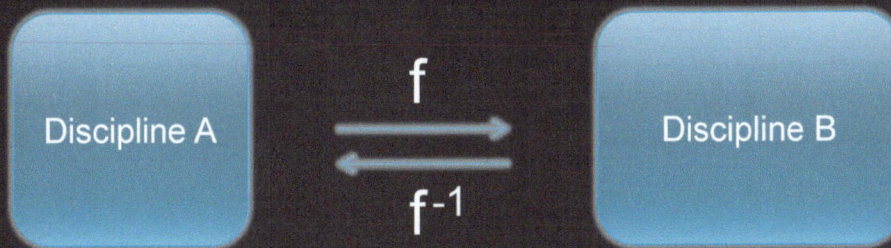

Extension of a metaphor can be thought as a function which projects vocabulary, ideas, theories and methods from one discipline to another and enriches both. I personally rediscovered isomorphism between systems several years ago and called it a metaphorical bijection.

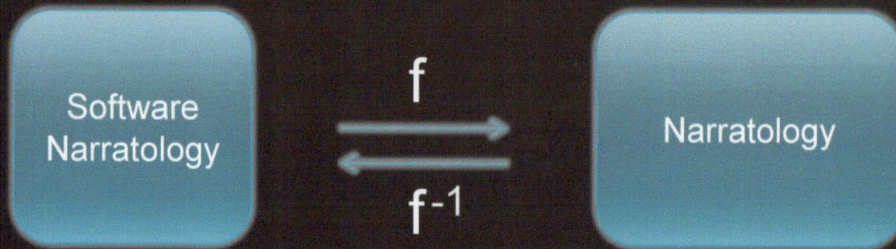

The new disciplines can be created in such a manner. As an example I repeat here software narratology that covers all types of narratives in software construction and post-construction phases.

Complementarity (Artifacts)

Quantum Mechanics and observables: x / p_x

Memory Dump / Software Trace

© 2012 Software Diagnostics Services

One of the general system-properties is the notion of complementarity where two or more independent things improve our diagnostics abilities. In software diagnostics we have Memory Dump vs. Software Traces. As noted previously, network traces are considered the same as software traces in principle.

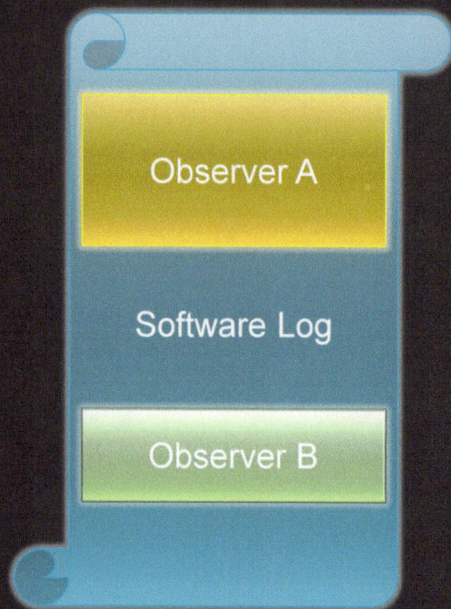

Complementarity (Reports)

Observer A

Software Log

Observer B

Solution: Pattern Checklists

In addition to software artifact complementarity there is also a complementarity of reports such as when several observers (or software diagnosticians) see different patterns. The obvious solution is to use checklists.

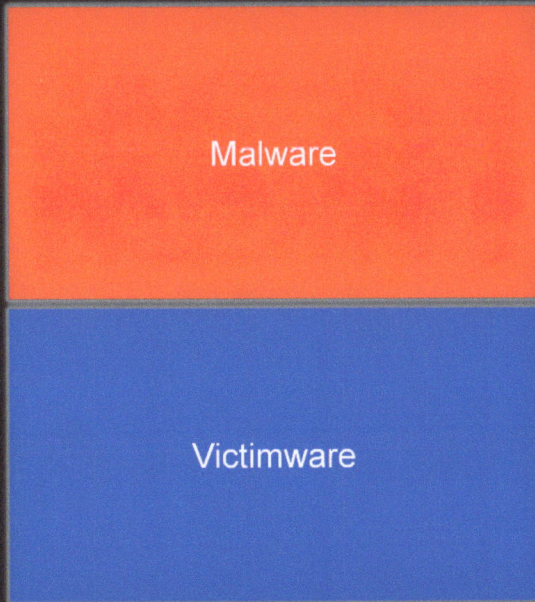

Here we mean Malware / Victimware dichotomy. You can find the reference to Victimware presentation on **Further Reading** slide later.

Decomposition of Behavior

- GUI state changes
- GUI messages
- Product specific messages
- System messages
- Memory dumps
- Network traces
- Screenshots

By decomposition of software behavior we mean using different tools to trace different aspects of software behavior simultaneously in order to reduce diagnostics artifact complexity.

Holistic Approach

- ⊙ Complete (or <u>fiber bundled</u>) dump

  - All processes and threads

- ⊙ Full trace

  - All modules

Systemic approaches are often associated with holism where the whole sum is more than the sum of its parts. Even if we use different tools for tracing different aspects we should strive to record all possible events and use artifact analysis tools to do filtering for us later. In such cases we minimize an impact of not recording important events especially for first fault cases.

Fiber bundled memory dump:
http://www.dumpanalysis.org/blog/index.php/2009/07/12/fiber-bundle-of-memory-space/

Diagnostics Complexity

Memory Dump Analysis

$$C \sim F\left(C_{Mem},\ C^{-1}_{Tool},\ C^{-1}_{Pat}\right)$$

C_{Mem} structural complexity

C_{Tool} the number of commands

C_{Pat} the number of patterns in a catalog

Another notion that arises in systems science is the so called complexity. Here we provide an example relation for memory dump analysis. For memory dumps the complexity (or diagnostics difficulty) depends on structural complexity (the number of components and their relationships), the number of diagnostics tools and their commands, and the number of patterns in a catalog. The more patterns we have the better, the more tools and commands we have the easier is diagnosis. For example, GDB has less number of commands, so to make the diagnostics effective the same as WinDbg debugger from Debugging Tools for Windows we have to use additional tools such as *vmmap* and diagnostic reports in addition to core dumps.

First Fault Diagnosis

- Most diagnostic patterns are first fault

- First fault vs. second fault tools

Software diagnostics is also a first fault software problem tool because patterns are first fault. Of course it depends on whether artifacts are collected on the first fault occurrence or not. I put here a link to a book by Dan Skwire that first pointed to me such important distinction.

First fault vs. second fault tools:

http://www.dumpanalysis.org/First+Fault+Software+Problem+Solving

Software Diagnostics Tools

Software Diagnostics Workbench

Software Diagnostics Services plans to release a workbench tool to help with day-to-day software diagnostics tasks.

Software Diagnostics Workbench:

http://www.dumpanalysis.com/software-diagnostics-workbench

I rarely make jokes during presentations. However, today we have an example of my abnormal behavior. Here is a systems joke: **M**hole in a **W**hole (moles or memory holes). It has to do with parallels with intelligence analysis via HUMINT and SIGINT.

Further Reading

Systems Thinking and Science

- An Introduction to General Systems Thinking (by Weinberg)
- Facets of Systems Science (by Klir)

Software Diagnostics

- Software Diagnostics Institute
- Memory Dump Analysis Anthology: Volumes 1, 2, 3, 4, 5, 6, 7, …
- Software Trace and Memory Dump Analysis: Patterns, Tools, Processes and Best Practices
- Introduction to Pattern-Driven Software Problem Solving
- Introduction to Software Narratology
- Introduction to Pattern-Driven Software Diagnostics
- Victimware

Software Diagnostics Institute:
http://www.dumpanalysis.org

Memory Dump Analysis Anthology: Volumes 1 - 6:
http://www.dumpanalysis.com/ ultimate-memory-analysis-reference

Software Trace and Memory Dump Analysis: Patterns, Tools, Processes and Best Practices:
http://www.dumpanalysis.com/STMDA-materials

Introduction to Pattern-Driven Software Problem Solving:
http://www.dumpanalysis.com/PDSPSI-materials

Introduction to Software Narratology:
http://www.dumpanalysis.com/Introduction-Software-Narratology-materials

Introduction to Pattern-Driven Software Diagnostics:
http://www.dumpanalysis.com/Introduction-Software-Diagnostics-materials

Victimware:
http://www.dumpanalysis.com/Victimware-materials

Next Webinar

Patterns → Explanations

Abductive Reasoning in Software Diagnostics

December, 2012

© 2012 Software Diagnostics Services

Next planned Webinar will be focused on abductive reasoning where consequences are used to infer possible and most likely explanations that guide further troubleshooting and debugging efforts. We also cover the difference between abduction, deduction and induction.

Pattern-Based
Software Diagnostics
Introduction

Version 1.0

Dmitry Vostokov
Software Diagnostics Services

Published by OpenTask, Republic of Ireland

OpenTask books and magazines are available through booksellers and distributors worldwide. For further information or comments send requests to press@opentask.com.

A CIP catalogue record for this book is available from the British Library.

ISBN-l3: 978-1-908043-49-8 (Paperback)

First printing, 2013

Pattern-Based
Software Diagnostics
Introduction

Version 1.0

Dmitry Vostokov
Software Diagnostics Services

Hello Everyone, my name is Dmitry Vostokov and I introduce pattern-based software diagnostics today. I decided to keep this presentation short and as simple as possible. If anything needs to be added or modified in the future I create another version of it

These prerequisites are very simple and I suppose you all like me enjoy diagnosing software problems, troubleshooting and debugging.

Software Diagnostics

A discipline studying abnormal software structure and behavior in software execution artifacts (such as memory dumps, software and network traces and logs) using **pattern-driven**, **systemic** and **pattern-based** analysis methodologies.

First, I would like to remind you a definition of software diagnostics we put forward in one of our previous webinars. Originally it only included pattern-driven and systemic analysis methodologies. We recently added pattern-based part. What it is about I hope you learn during this presentation.

Pattern-driven:
http://www.patterndiagnostics.com/Introduction-Software-Diagnostics-materials

Systemic:
http://www.patterndiagnostics.com/systemic-diagnostics-materials

Pattern-based:
http://www.dumpanalysis.org/pattern-based-software-diagnostics

Diagnostics Pattern

A common recurrent identifiable problem together with **a set of recommendations** and **possible** solutions to apply in a specific context.

Next we would like to mention a definition of a software diagnostics pattern. There are some differences with a usual definition of a pattern from software construction such as architectural and design patterns. The difference is that often upon a diagnostic encounter we provide recommendations and possible solutions instead of just problem solutions.

Pattern Orientation

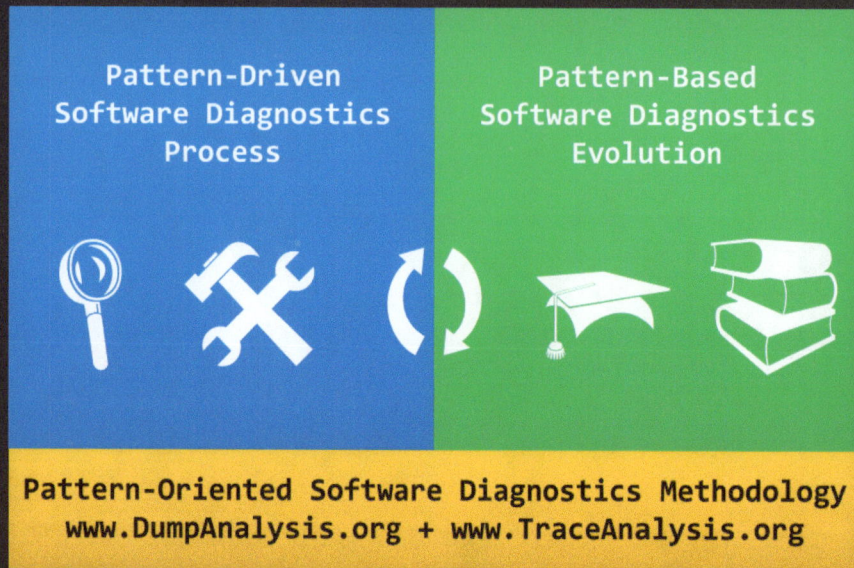

So you see that software diagnostics is about patterns and pattern recognition. Let's say it is pattern-oriented and includes pattern-based and pattern-driven parts. Pattern-driven is about diagnostics process and pattern-based is about pattern life cycle. We first start with the pattern-driven part.

Pattern-Driven

- Finding patterns in software artefacts

- Using checklists and pattern catalogs

To repeat, pattern-driven means finding patterns of abnormal structure and behavior in software execution artifacts such memory dumps, software logs and network traces. To help with this there are checklists and pattern catalogs (and tools of course).

There are so many identified patterns that I dubbed this present situation as a pattern cloud. One way to make this cloud helpful is to have several pattern catalogs.

Pattern Catalogs

- Classification

- Partition

A pattern catalog is just a collection of patterns according to some criteria. So we first classify catalogs and then partition them into sections for easy navigation and search.

Catalog Classification

- ⊙ **By abstraction**

  Meta-patterns

- ⊙ **By artefact type**

  Software Log   Memory Dump   Network Trace

- ⊙ **By story type**

  Problem Description   Software Disruption   UI Problem

- ⊙ **By intention**

  Malware

We can classify catalogs by abstraction, for example, as software diagnostics meta-patterns which are patterns of software diagnostics itself. Then we can classify catalogs by the type of software execution artifacts, such as software traces and logs, memory dumps and network traces. Another classification is by a story type, such as by problem descriptions, by software disruptions, and by user interface problems. Also we can separate patterns by intention such as malware (with unintentional patterns, the rest, all grouped as Victimware).

Meta-patterns:

http://www.dumpanalysis.org/blog/index.php/2012/06/09/patterns-of-software-diagnostics-part-1/

Software Log:

http://www.dumpanalysis.org/blog/index.php/trace-analysis-patterns/

Memory Dump:

http://www.dumpanalysis.org/blog/index.php/crash-dump-analysis-patterns/

Network Trace:

http://www.dumpanalysis.org/blog/index.php/2012/07/19/network-trace-analysis-patterns-part-1/

Problem Description:

http://www.dumpanalysis.org/blog/index.php/2012/03/11/software-problem-description-patterns-part-1/

Software Disruption:

http://www.dumpanalysis.org/blog/index.php/2013/01/12/software-disruption-patterns-part-1/

UI Problem:

http://www.dumpanalysis.org/blog/index.php/user-interface-problem-analysis-patterns/

Malware:

http://www.dumpanalysis.org/blog/index.php/malware-analysis-patterns/

Catalog Partition

- By execution mode and space

- By reported problem type

  Crash   Hang   Spike   Leak

- By structure and behavior

  Structural memory patterns   Software trace classification

- By objects

  Thread   Process   Module   Exception   Stack Trace

- By actions

  Wait Chain   Contention   Deadlock

Some catalogs become large and need partitioning. Memory dump analysis pattern catalog, for example, consists of more than 250 patterns; software log analysis pattern catalog consists of more than 60 patterns. For example, we can partition memory dump analysis patterns by execution space or problem type, such as crash, hang, spike or leak. We can also partition them by structure and behavior, for example, to create a smaller catalog for structural memory patterns. Another fruitful partition is by object types such as threads, processes, modules, exceptions, stack traces or by actions such as various wait chains, resource contentions, deadlocks and livelocks. Software trace analysis pattern catalog is based on structural software narratology.

Execution mode and space (incomplete):

http://www.dumpanalysis.org/blog/index.php/2008/07/21/cda-pattern-classification-spacemode/

Structural memory patterns:

http://www.dumpanalysis.org/blog/index.php/2008/07/21/cda-pattern-classification-spacemode/

Software trace classification:

http://www.patterndiagnostics.com/Training/Accelerated-Windows-Software-Trace-Analysis-Public.pdf

Thread:

http://www.dumpanalysis.org/blog/index.php/2013/01/05/thread-patterns/

Process:

http://www.dumpanalysis.org/blog/index.php/2013/01/05/process-patterns/

Module:

http://www.dumpanalysis.org/blog/index.php/2012/07/15/module-patterns/

Exception:

http://www.dumpanalysis.org/blog/index.php/2011/11/29/exception-patterns/

Stack Trace:

http://www.dumpanalysis.org/blog/index.php/2011/06/18/stack-trace-patterns/

Wait Chain:

http://www.dumpanalysis.org/blog/index.php/2009/02/17/wait-chain-patterns/

Contention:

http://www.dumpanalysis.org/blog/index.php/2010/09/21/contention-patterns/

Deadlock:

http://www.dumpanalysis.org/blog/index.php/2009/02/17/deadlock-patterns/

Ultimately patterns are found on specific platforms. By pattern implementation we mean diagnostics differences in different operating systems and product lines.

Mac OS X:
http://www.dumpanalysis.org/blog/index.php/category/mac-os-x/

Pattern Form

- Description

- Description + Recommendation

- Description + Solution

Now I say a few words about forms of software diagnostics patterns. Based on pattern definition we propose at least 3 forms here. These should be fairly intuitive.

Pattern Networks

- [Intra-Catalog](#)

- [Inter-Catalog](#)

Of course, patterns are not diagnosed in isolation and they form networks. Such networks can be intra-catalog (originally called pattern interaction or cooperation) such as associated patterns in memory dumps or software logs or inter-catalog such between user interface problem patterns, software traces and memory dumps, for example.

Intra-Catalog:
http://www.dumpanalysis.org/blog/index.php/pattern-cooperation/

Inter-Catalog:
http://www.debuggingexperts.com/memory-dump-trace-analysis-unified-pattern-approach

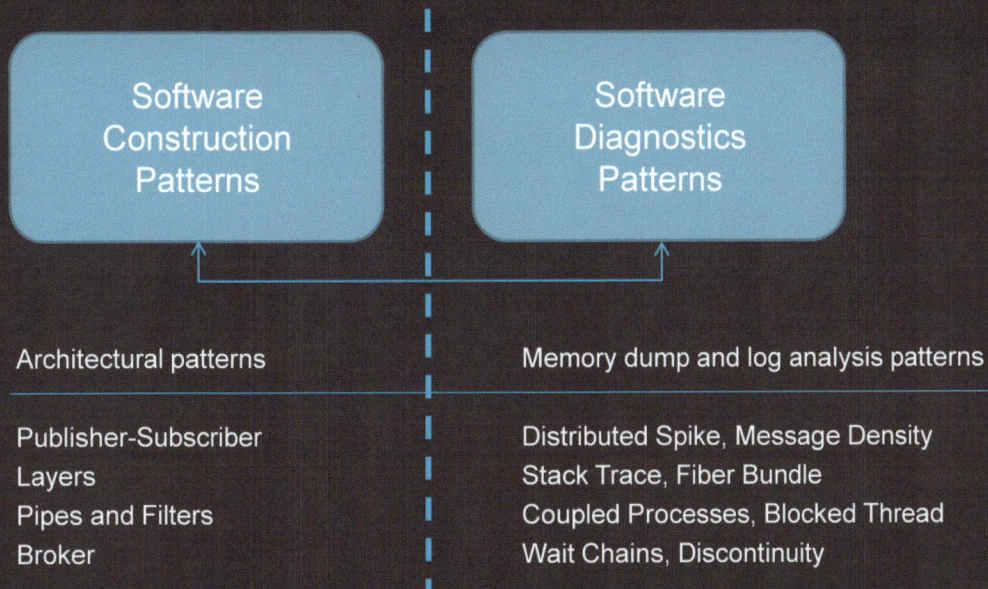

Most software architects I talked to think that architecture and low-level memory contents are separate things from different layers of abstraction. Fortunately, it is now possible to connect them through patterns as you can see on this picture. We can also map design and implementation patterns and idioms to patterns of software behaviour and the other way around. One example of implementation mapping is static code analysis patterns and I put a link on this slide.

Static Code Analysis Patterns:

http://www.dumpanalysis.org/blog/index.php/category/static-code-analysis-patterns/

Pattern Sequences

- Originally: Pattern Succession

- Inter-Catalog

Now I say a few words about pattern sequences. These are more specialized forms of pattern networks and are sets of patterns that have definite causal links. Looking at software diagnostics cases it is easy to see that some patterns precede others, for example, heap corruption causes an error message box and then blocks other threads, creating conditions for another pattern to appear, wait chains. Blocked threads may block other coupled processes creating inter-process wait chains and finally inter-machine wait chains. Some patterns are most likely found in succession and other patterns are less likely to effect abnormal conditions. Such pattern sequences can help in troubleshooting, debugging and root cause analysis.

Pattern Succession:
http://www.dumpanalysis.org/blog/index.php/2010/06/03/succession-of-patterns-part-2/

Inter-Catalog:
http://www.dumpanalysis.org/blog/index.php/2009/06/22/succession-of-patterns-part-1/

Pattern-Based

- Pattern evolution

- Catalog evolution

- Catalog distibution

What is under the umbrella of pattern-based part such as pattern and pattern catalogue evolution was implicit in our definition of software diagnostics that was initially just called pattern-driven. However, the recognition of pattern-based part in software design engineering led to explicit naming of this part in software diagnostics.

Catalog Evolution

- Finding new patterns in artefacts

- Pattern prediction

- Pattern split

- Pattern unification

- New catalogs

Of course, like medical diagnostics, software diagnostics is evolving. New recurrent patterns are constantly found in artefacts and described. This is one way to expand pattern catalogues. Another way is to predict patterns based on pattern implementation. For example, if we find a new pattern in Mac OS X core dump we should assess if the same kind of a pattern exists or possible in Windows memory dumps. Another example is network trace analysis patterns that can be predicted from more general software trace analysis patterns. Other ways of pattern evolution are pattern splits when one pattern becomes too general and pattern unification when we have many specializations that differ only in minor details. And sometimes it is possible to create entirely new catalogues as was recently done with software disruption patterns.

Pattern-prediction:
http://www.dumpanalysis.org/blog/index.php/2012/04/28/software-behavior-pattern-prediction/

New catalogs:
http://www.dumpanalysis.org/blog/index.php/2013/01/12/software-disruption-patterns-part-1/

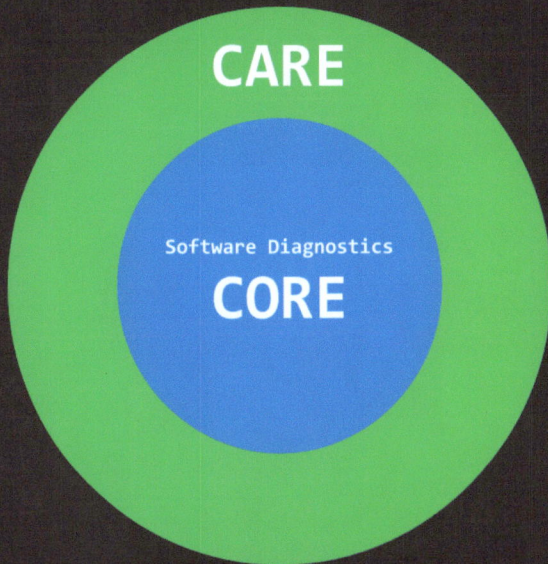

Now I say a word about tools. Software Diagnostics Services is working on Software Diagnostics Workbench with nicely formatted pattern catalogs having easy navigation, explanations, revised and extended command to pattern maps, typical software diagnostics case studies and lots of other practical information..

Software Diagnostics Workbench:
http://www.dumpanalysis.com/software-diagnostics-workbench

Economic Benefits

- Improved communication of diagnostics reports using uniform pattern language
- Increased productivity by systematic pattern usage
- Increased quality by leveraging existing expertise
- Support for global teams
- Quantifiable analysis

We hope that pattern-oriented software diagnostics has tangible economic benefits as well including quantifiable analysis such the number of patterns searched and the number identified.

Further Reading

Pattern-Based Software Construction

- *"Pattern-Oriented Software Architecture: A System of Patterns"*
  by Frank Buschmann, Regine Meunier, Hans Rohnert, Peter Sommerlad, Michael Stal
- *"Pattern-Oriented Software Architecture: On Pattern and Pattern Languages"*
  by Frank Buschmann, Kevlin Henney, Douglas C. Schmidt
- *"Patterns-Based Engineering: Successfully Delivering Solutions via Patterns"*
  by Lee Ackerman, Celso Gonzalez

Pattern-Based Software Diagnostics

- Software Diagnostics Institute
- Memory Dump Analysis Anthology: Volumes 1, 2, 3, 4, 5, 6, 7, 8, ...
  Volume 6 is in preparation (January, 2013)
  Volume 7 is in preparation (February, 2013)
  Volume 8 is planned for November, 2013
- Software Trace and Memory Dump Analysis: Patterns, Tools, Processes and Best Practices
- Introduction to Pattern-Driven Software Problem Solving
- Software Trace and Memory Dump Analysis
- Introduction to Pattern-Driven Software Diagnostics

The first book from software construction list is about architectural patterns I mentioned on the slide about the great divide. The second book is very useful as an introduction to construction patterns in general and some ideas are applicable to post-construction phase too. The third book on patterns-based software engineering is focused on software construction too and prompted me to add pattern life cycle to software diagnostics. I also included links to relevant presentations and books focused on software post-construction phase including software diagnostics, troubleshooting and debugging.

Software Diagnostics Institute:
http://www.dumpanalysis.org

Memory Dump Analysis Anthology volumes:
http://www.patterndiagnostics.com/ultimate-memory-analysis-reference

Software Trace and Memory Dump Analysis: Patterns, Tools, Processes and Best Practices:
http://www.patterndiagnostics.com/STMDA-materials

Introduction to Pattern-Driven Software Problem Solving:
http://www.patterndiagnostics.com/PDSPSI-materials

Software Trace and Memory Dump Analysis:
http://www.patterndiagnostics.com/STMDA-materials

Introduction to Pattern-Driven Software Diagnostics:
http://www.patterndiagnostics.com/Introduction-Software-Diagnostics-materials

A Bit of Philosophy

If want to be the best software diagnostician you need to be a philosopher.

After Galen's thoughts on medicine

Introduction to Philosophy of Software Diagnostics

© 2013 Software Diagnostics Services

Our next free webinar is on philosophy of software diagnostics. The great Roman physician and philosopher Galen once said that to be the best medic you need to be a philosopher. So the same we believe is true for software diagnostics.

Introduction to Philosophy of Software Diagnostics:

http://www.patterndiagnostics.com/philosophy-software-diagnostics-introduction

Victimware

The Missing Part of the Equation

Version 1.0

Dmitry Vostokov
Software Diagnostics Services

Published by OpenTask, Republic of Ireland

OpenTask books and magazines are available through booksellers and distributors worldwide. For further information or comments send requests to press@opentask.com.

A CIP catalogue record for this book is available from the British Library.

ISBN-l3: 978-1-908043-63-4 (Paperback)

First printing, 2013

Victimware
The Missing Part of the Equation

Version 1.0

Dmitry Vostokov
Software Diagnostics Services

Hello everyone, my name is Dmitry Vostokov and I introduce Victimware presentation today. This is a version one of the Webinar. If I missed anything during preparation I add it to the version 2. At the end of my preparation I decided to keep this presentation as simple as possible and as short as possible and add a practical example at the end.

The prerequisites are interest in software diagnostics, malware detection and analysis.

Goal

Make malware research and analysis community aware of pattern-driven software diagnostics

This Webinar has a simple goal: to introduce pattern-driven software diagnostics to malware research and analysis community.

What is Victimware?

Victimware

Malware

Definition: Software affected by execution behavior of other components.

© 2012 Software Diagnostics Services

Victimware can be defined as software whose execution is affected by execution behavior of other components. The latter is broad enough to include software causing unintentional problems and even software that is supposed to protect from malware. We also included Malware in Victimware box because malware can also suffer the same behavioral problems as its intentional and unintentional victims.

Why Victimware?

Victimology

Software Victimology

Victim thread in Mac OS X

There are some parallels between victims of crimes and victims of malware. For example, the focus of public attention is usually more on criminals and malware (or crimeware part of malware) and less on victims and victimware despite the fact that the latter include the largest part of the population and software components.

Typology of Victimware

Modified Schafer's functional typology:

- Targeted
- Unrelated
- Self-Victimized
- Provocative (Impelementation- and design-weak)
- Precipitative (inappropriate data communication)
- Political (empires of code)

Now I say a few words about victimware typology. Here I borrowed the typology from Schafer (a well-known victimologist) and modified it a little. Some types are obvious. Provocative victimware is software that due to its implementation and design flaws attracts malware writers. Precipitative victimware is software which communicates inappropriate data despite being well designed and implemented so the focus of responsibility shifts to software users. Political victimware is a victim of battles between various software vendors. Here a typical example would be various value-adding components.

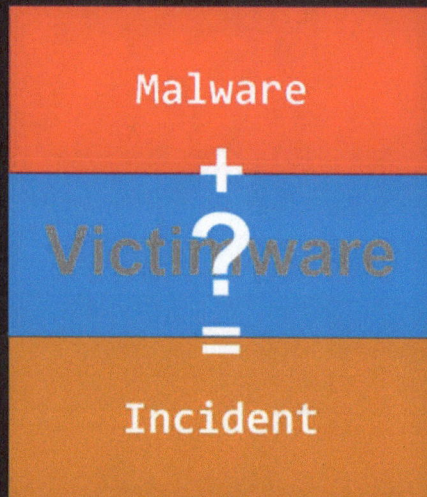

The approach of software victimology is to use patterns of abnormal software behavior such as crashes, hangs, spikes, leaks, patching and so on to discover malware.

Behavioral Patterns

...

Heap Corruption

Wild Code

Hooked Functions

Activity Resonance

Deviant Module

...

http://www.dumpanalysis.org/blog/index.php/crash-dump-analysis-patterns/

© 2012 Software Diagnostics Services

There are more than two hundred software behavior patterns that can be found on Software Diagnostics Institute website. Some of them you would see during the practical example at the end of this presentation.

http://www.dumpanalysis.org/blog/index.php/crash-dump-analysis-patterns/

Structural Patterns

...

Memory Region

Region Boundary

Module

Stack

...

http://www.dumpanalysis.org/blog/index.php/structural-memory-analysis-patterns/

Some patterns are related to the organization of memory and they are in the process of development:

http://www.dumpanalysis.org/blog/index.php/structural-memory-analysis-patterns

Practice

Crash Dump Analysis Example

© 2012 Software Diagnostics Services

Now comes the practical part. A user noticed IE crashing from time to time and set up the system to save user process crash dumps. So we look at one of them.

Annotated log file from WinDbg session

We setup up symbols first:

```
0:005> .symfix c:\mss
```

```
0:005> .reload
.................................................
....................................
Loading unloaded module list
..
```

The stack trace shows heap corruption that triggered exception processing. We also see a raw pointer **0x4aaaf**:

```
0:005> k
ChildEBP RetAddr
02aec974 77655620 ntdll!KiFastSystemCallRet
02aec978 77683c62 ntdll!NtWaitForSingleObject+0xc
02aec9fc 77683d4b ntdll!RtlReportExceptionEx+0x14b
02aeca3c 7769fa87 ntdll!RtlReportException+0x3c
02aeca50 7769fb0d ntdll!RtlpTerminateFailureFilter+0x14
02aeca5c 775f9bdc ntdll!RtlReportCriticalFailure+0x6b
02aeca70 775f4067 ntdll!_EH4_CallFilterFunc+0x12
02aeca98 77655f79 ntdll!_except_handler4+0x8e
02aecabc 77655f4b ntdll!ExecuteHandler2+0x26
02aecb6c 77655dd7 ntdll!ExecuteHandler+0x24
02aecb6c 7769faf8 ntdll!KiUserExceptionDispatcher+0xf
02aecee0 776a0704 ntdll!RtlReportCriticalFailure+0x5b
02aecef0 776a07f2 ntdll!RtlpReportHeapFailure+0x21
02aecf24 7766b1a5 ntdll!RtlpLogHeapFailure+0xa1
02aecf6c 7765730a ntdll!RtlpCoalesceFreeBlocks+0x4b9
02aed064 77657545 ntdll!RtlpFreeHeap+0x1e2
02aed080 75e47e4b ntdll!RtlFreeHeap+0x14e
02aed0c8 77037277 kernel32!GlobalFree+0x47
02aed0dc 774b4a1f ole32!ReleaseStgMedium+0x124 [d:\longhorn\com\ole32\ole232\base\api.cpp @ 964]
02aed0f0 77517feb urlmon!ReleaseBindInfo+0x4c
02aed100 774d9a87 urlmon!CINet::ReleaseCNetObjects+0x3d
02aed118 774d93f0 urlmon!CINetHttp::OnWininetRequestHandleClosing+0x60
02aed12c 76432078 urlmon!CINet::CINetCallback+0x2de
02aed274 76438f5d wininet!InternetIndicateStatus+0xfc
02aed2a4 7643937a wininet!HANDLE_OBJECT::~HANDLE_OBJECT+0xc9
02aed2c0 7643916b wininet!INTERNET_CONNECT_HANDLE_OBJECT::~INTERNET_CONNECT_HANDLE_OBJECT+0x209
02aed2cc 76438d5e wininet!HTTP_REQUEST_HANDLE_OBJECT::`vector deleting destructor'+0xd
02aed2dc 76434e72 wininet!HANDLE_OBJECT::Dereference+0x22
02aed2e8 76439419 wininet!DereferenceObject+0x21
02aed310 76439114 wininet!_InternetCloseHandle+0x9d
02aed330 0004aaaf wininet!InternetCloseHandle+0x11e
WARNING: Frame IP not in any known module. Following frames may be wrong.
02aed33c 774c5d25 0x4aaaf
02aed358 774c5d95 urlmon!CINet::TerminateRequest+0x82
02aed364 774c5d7c urlmon!CINet::MyUnlockRequest+0x10
02aed370 774c5d63 urlmon!CINetProtImpl::UnlockRequest+0x10
02aed37c 774c5d49 urlmon!CINetEmbdFilter::UnlockRequest+0x11
02aed388 774b743d urlmon!CINet::UnlockRequest+0x13
02aed394 774b73e1 urlmon!COInetProt::UnlockRequest+0x11
02aed3a8 774b7530 urlmon!CTransaction::UnlockRequest+0x36
02aed3b4 774b74e0 urlmon!CTransData::~CTransData+0x3a
```

```
02aed3c0 774b74c9 urlmon!CTransData::`scalar deleting destructor'+0xd
02aed3d8 774e221f urlmon!CTransData::Release+0x25
02aed3e0 774b6d0a urlmon!CReadOnlyStreamDirect::~CReadOnlyStreamDirect+0x1a
02aed3ec 774b7319 urlmon!CReadOnlyStreamDirect::`vector deleting destructor'+0xd
02aed404 774b72be urlmon!CReadOnlyStreamDirect::Release+0x25
02aed410 774b71f4 urlmon!CBinding::~CBinding+0xb9
02aed41c 774b71dd urlmon!CBinding::`scalar deleting destructor'+0xd
02aed434 6b20b0e8 urlmon!CBinding::Release+0x25
02aed448 6b20b0ba mshtml!ATL::AtlComPtrAssign+0x2b
02aed458 6b20b8de mshtml!ATL::CComPtr<IBindCallbackInternal>::operator=+0x15
02aed464 6b20b8aa mshtml!CBindingXSSFilter::TearDown+0x2b
02aed46c 6b20b887 mshtml!BindingXSSFilter_TearDown+0x19
02aed478 6b0da61a mshtml!CStreamProxy::Passivate+0x12
02aed484 6b0ddf3a mshtml!CBaseFT::Release+0x1d
02aed4ac 6b0e0b70 mshtml!CDwnBindData::TerminateBind+0x11d
02aed4b8 6b11a2a9 mshtml!CDwnBindData::TerminateOnApt+0x14
02aed4ec 6b105066 mshtml!GlobalWndOnMethodCall+0xfb
02aed50c 7742fd72 mshtml!GlobalWndProc+0x183
02aed538 7742fe4a user32!InternalCallWinProc+0x23
02aed5b0 7743018d user32!UserCallWinProcCheckWow+0x14b
02aed614 7743022b user32!DispatchMessageWorker+0x322
02aed624 6ecac1d5 user32!DispatchMessageW+0xf
02aef72c 6ec5337e ieframe!CTabWindow::_TabWindowThreadProc+0x54c
02aef7e4 760f426d ieframe!LCIETab_ThreadProc+0x2c1
02aef7f4 75e4d0e9 iertutil!CIsoScope::RegisterThread+0xab
02aef800 776319bb kernel32!BaseThreadInitThunk+0xe
02aef840 7763198e ntdll!__RtlUserThreadStart+0x23
02aef858 00000000 ntdll!_RtlUserThreadStart+0x1b
```

We check the return address for the raw pointer and it seems to be valid (show a *call* instruction):

```
0:005> ub 774c5d25
urlmon!CINet::TerminateRequest+0x5d:
774c5d0d 8bde            mov     ebx,esi
774c5d0f ff75fc          push    dword ptr [ebp-4]
774c5d12 ff15b0174b77    call    dword ptr [urlmon!_imp__LeaveCriticalSection (774b17b0)]
774c5d18 85ff            test    edi,edi
774c5d1a 8b355d4a0577    mov     esi,dword ptr [urlmon!_imp__InternetCloseHandle (7757a0d4)]
774c5d20 7403            je      urlmon!CINet::TerminateRequest+0x82 (774c5d25)
774c5d22 57              push    edi
774c5d23 ffd6            call    esi
```

The call is indirect and we check its target:

```
0:005> dps 7757a0d4 L1
7757a0d4  76439088 wininet!InternetCloseHandle
```

If we disassemble the target we see it was patched with a jump:

```
0:005> u 76439088
wininet!InternetCloseHandle:
76439088 e9031ac189      jmp     0004aa90
7643908d 51              push    ecx
7643908e 51              push    ecx
7643908f 53              push    ebx
76439090 56              push    esi
76439091 57              push    edi
76439092 33db            xor     ebx,ebx
76439094 33ff            xor     edi,edi
```

If we follow the jump destination and disassemble it we find valid code:

```
0:005> u 0004aa90
0004aa90 55              push    ebp
0004aa91 8bec            mov     ebp,esp
0004aa93 837d0800        cmp     dword ptr [ebp+8],0
0004aa97 740c            je      0004aaa5
0004aa99 8b4508          mov     eax,dword ptr [ebp+8]
0004aa9c 50              push    eax
0004aa9d e82eedffff      call    000497d0
0004aaa2 83c404          add     esp,4
```

However the address is not among the loaded modules:

```
0:005> lm
start    end      module name
00340000 003dc000  iexplore   (deferred)
023b0000 023bb000  msimtf     (deferred)
16080000 160a5000  mdnsNSP    (deferred)
6ab50000 6ab76000  dssenh     (deferred)
6b030000 6b5e0000  mshtml     (pdb symbols)
c:\mss\mshtml.pdb\45662F54BF3247F1B5694A9B5794CDA32\mshtml.pdb
6ba10000 6bac4000  jscript    (deferred)
6cec0000 6cedb000  cryptnet   (deferred)
6d260000 6d26e000  pngfilt    (deferred)
6d2f0000 6d319000  msls31     (deferred)
6d700000 6d730000  mlang      (deferred)
6d740000 6d78d000  ssv        (deferred)
6d7b0000 6d7bc000  imgutil    (deferred)
6ddb0000 6dddf000  iepeers    (deferred)
6df20000 6df53000  IEShims    (deferred)
6eb80000 6f614000  ieframe    (pdb symbols)
c:\mss\ieframe.pdb\E6F6B77F09704E24904C82F5746BA46D2\ieframe.pdb
703b0000 70403000  actxprxy   (deferred)
70740000 70780000  ieproxy    (deferred)
725a0000 725b2000  pnrpnsp    (deferred)
725d0000 725d8000  winrnr     (deferred)
725e0000 72716000  msxml3     (deferred)
72720000 7272c000  wshbth     (deferred)
72730000 7273f000  NapiNSP    (deferred)
72890000 72896000  SensApi    (deferred)
72ec0000 72f02000  winspool   (deferred)
734b0000 734b6000  rasadhlp   (deferred)
736b0000 73735000  comctl32_736b0000   (deferred)
73ac0000 73ac7000  midimap    (deferred)
73ae0000 73af4000  msacm32_73ae0000    (deferred)
73b00000 73b66000  AudioEng   (deferred)
73c30000 73c39000  msacm32    (deferred)
73c60000 73c81000  AudioSes   (deferred)
73c90000 73cbf000  wdmaud     (deferred)
74290000 7434b000  propsys    (deferred)
74390000 7439f000  nlaapi     (deferred)
743a0000 743a4000  ksuser     (deferred)
74430000 74445000  cabinet    (deferred)
74450000 7448d000  oleacc     (deferred)
74490000 7463b000  GdiPlus    (deferred)
74640000 74668000  MMDevAPI   (deferred)
74670000 746a2000  winmm      (deferred)
746b0000 746e1000  tapi32     (deferred)
749e0000 74b7e000  comctl32   (deferred)
```

```
74b80000 74b87000   avrt        (deferred)
74ba0000 74bea000   rasapi32    (deferred)
74ce0000 74d1f000   uxtheme     (deferred)
74de0000 74e0d000   wintrust    (deferred)
74ea0000 74eb4000   rasman      (deferred)
74f70000 74f7c000   rtutils     (deferred)
74f80000 74f85000   WSHTCPIP    (deferred)
74fb0000 74fd1000   ntmarta     (deferred)
75010000 7504b000   rsaenh      (deferred)
75050000 75055000   msimg32     (deferred)
75060000 75075000   gpapi       (deferred)
750a0000 750e6000   schannel    (deferred)
752b0000 752eb000   mswsock     (deferred)
75370000 753b5000   bcrypt      (deferred)
753f0000 753f5000   wship6      (deferred)
75400000 75408000   version     (deferred)
75420000 75427000   credssp     (deferred)
75430000 75465000   ncrypt      (deferred)
75480000 754a2000   dhcpcsvc6   (deferred)
754b0000 754b7000   winnsi      (deferred)
754c0000 754f5000   dhcpcsvc    (deferred)
75500000 75519000   IPHLPAPI    (deferred)
75590000 755ca000   SLC         (deferred)
755d0000 756c2000   crypt32     (deferred)
75740000 75752000   msasn1      (deferred)
75760000 75771000   samlib      (deferred)
75780000 757f6000   netapi32    (deferred)
75800000 7582c000   dnsapi      (deferred)
75a70000 75acf000   sxs         (deferred)
75ad0000 75afc000   apphelp     (deferred)
75b30000 75b44000   secur32     (deferred)
75b50000 75b6e000   userenv     (deferred)
75c90000 75c97000   psapi       (deferred)
75ca0000 75d63000   rpcrt4      (deferred)
75d70000 75de3000   comdlg32    (deferred)
75df0000 75df9000   lpk         (deferred)
75e00000 75edc000   kernel32    (pdb symbols)
c:\mss\kernel32.pdb\FCCF6FAC09804D49A4BB256A77F519572\kernel32.pdb
75ee0000 75f8a000   msvcrt      (deferred)
75f90000 76178000   iertutil    (pdb symbols)
c:\mss\iertutil.pdb\6ACF7EBB19D84A2CAF858A4AB2BE87D42\iertutil.pdb
76180000 761a9000   imagehlp    (deferred)
761b0000 761b6000   nsi         (deferred)
761c0000 76244000   clbcatq     (deferred)
76250000 76299000   Wldap32     (deferred)
762a0000 76366000   advapi32    (deferred)
76370000 763bb000   gdi32       (deferred)
763c0000 76419000   shlwapi     (deferred)
76420000 76506000   wininet     (pdb symbols)
c:\mss\wininet.pdb\59602CF9943B4634BAF101ED3FD999592\wininet.pdb
76510000 77020000   shell32     (deferred)
77020000 77165000   ole32       (private pdb symbols)
c:\mss\ole32.pdb\4F6EE07E85D24C1782E71BDDFD6CABC52\ole32.pdb
77170000 771ed000   usp10       (deferred)
771f0000 7727d000   oleaut32    (deferred)
77280000 7740a000   setupapi    (deferred)
77410000 774ad000   user32      (pdb symbols)
c:\mss\user32.pdb\CFD2C4C8EB9C406D8B6DC29512EB176A2\user32.pdb
774b0000 775e3000   urlmon      (pdb symbols)
c:\mss\urlmon.pdb\028B7E3D82774D4099DB238624D414C52\urlmon.pdb
```

```
775f0000 77717000   ntdll      (pdb symbols)
c:\mss\ntdll.pdb\2A581B1A8A244C51992668A826BF4FBB2\ntdll.pdb
77720000 77723000   normaliz   (deferred)
77730000 7775d000   ws2_32     (deferred)
77760000 7777e000   imm32      (deferred)
77780000 77848000   msctf      (deferred)
7c340000 7c396000   msvcr71    (deferred)

Unloaded modules:
75420000 75427000   credssp.dll
6b670000 6b693000   sqmapi.dll
```

If we look at its memory region attributes we see that it is a read-write execution region whereas normal code should be read-only:

```
0:005> !address 0004aa90
                              Failed to map Heaps (error 80004005)
Usage:                 <unclassified>
Allocation Base:       00040000
Base Address:          00040000
End Address:           0005d000
Region Size:           0001d000
Type:                  00020000 MEM_PRIVATE
State:                 00001000 MEM_COMMIT
Protect:               00000040 PAGE_EXECUTE_READWRITE
```

If we scan the process address range for any hidden modules we find our module plus the other one called *screens_dll.dll* that also has a different protection attribute compared to the rest of modules like iexplore.exe:

```
0:005> .imgscan
MZ at 00040000, prot 00000040, type 00020000 - size 1d000
MZ at 00340000, prot 00000002, type 01000000 - size 9c000
  Name: iexplore.exe
MZ at 02250000, prot 00000002, type 00040000 - size 2000
MZ at 023b0000, prot 00000002, type 01000000 - size b000
  Name: msimtf.dll
MZ at 03f80000, prot 00000002, type 00040000 - size 2000
MZ at 10000000, prot 00000004, type 00020000 - size 5000
  Name: screens_dll.dll
MZ at 16080000, prot 00000002, type 01000000 - size 25000
  Name: mdnsNSP.dll
MZ at 6ab50000, prot 00000002, type 01000000 - size 26000
  Name: DSSENH.dll
MZ at 6b030000, prot 00000002, type 01000000 - size 5b0000
  Name: MSHTML.dll
MZ at 6ba10000, prot 00000002, type 01000000 - size b4000
  Name: JSCRIPT.dll
MZ at 6cec0000, prot 00000002, type 01000000 - size 1b000
  Name: CRYPTNET.dll
MZ at 6d260000, prot 00000002, type 01000000 - size e000
  Name: PNGFILTER.DLL
MZ at 6d2f0000, prot 00000002, type 01000000 - size 29000
  Name: msls31.dll
MZ at 6d700000, prot 00000002, type 01000000 - size 30000
  Name: MLANG.dll
MZ at 6d740000, prot 00000002, type 01000000 - size 4d000
  Name: SSV.DLL
```

```
MZ at 6d7b0000, prot 00000002, type 01000000 - size c000
  Name: ImgUtil.dll
MZ at 6ddb0000, prot 00000002, type 01000000 - size 2f000
  Name: iepeers.DLL
MZ at 6df20000, prot 00000002, type 01000000 - size 33000
  Name: IEShims.dll
MZ at 6eb80000, prot 00000002, type 01000000 - size a94000
  Name: IEFRAME.dll
MZ at 703b0000, prot 00000002, type 01000000 - size 53000
  Name: SWEEPRX.dll
MZ at 70740000, prot 00000002, type 01000000 - size 40000
  Name: SWEEPRX.dll
MZ at 725a0000, prot 00000002, type 01000000 - size 12000
  Name: PNRPNSP.dll
MZ at 725d0000, prot 00000002, type 01000000 - size 8000
  Name: WINRNR.dll
MZ at 725e0000, prot 00000002, type 01000000 - size 136000
  Name: MSXML3.dll
MZ at 72720000, prot 00000002, type 01000000 - size c000
  Name: wshbth.dll
MZ at 72730000, prot 00000002, type 01000000 - size f000
  Name: NAPINSP.dll
MZ at 72890000, prot 00000002, type 01000000 - size 6000
  Name: SensApi.dll
MZ at 72ec0000, prot 00000002, type 01000000 - size 42000
  Name: WINSPOOL.DRV
MZ at 734b0000, prot 00000002, type 01000000 - size 6000
  Name: rasadhlp.dll
MZ at 736b0000, prot 00000002, type 01000000 - size 85000
  Name: COMCTL32.dll
MZ at 73ac0000, prot 00000002, type 01000000 - size 7000
  Name: MIDIMAP.dll
MZ at 73ae0000, prot 00000002, type 01000000 - size 14000
  Name: MSACM32.dll
MZ at 73b00000, prot 00000002, type 01000000 - size 66000
  Name: audioeng.dll
MZ at 73c30000, prot 00000002, type 01000000 - size 9000
  Name: MSACM32.DRV
MZ at 73c60000, prot 00000002, type 01000000 - size 21000
  Name: AudioSes.DLL
MZ at 73c90000, prot 00000002, type 01000000 - size 2f000
  Name: WINMMDRV.dll
MZ at 74290000, prot 00000002, type 01000000 - size bb000
  Name: PROPSYS.dll
MZ at 74390000, prot 00000002, type 01000000 - size f000
  Name: nlaapi.dll
MZ at 743a0000, prot 00000002, type 01000000 - size 4000
  Name: ksuser.dll
MZ at 74430000, prot 00000002, type 01000000 - size 15000
  Name: Cabinet.dll
MZ at 74450000, prot 00000002, type 01000000 - size 3d000
  Name: OLEACC.dll
MZ at 74490000, prot 00000002, type 01000000 - size 1ab000
  Name: gdiplus.dll
MZ at 74640000, prot 00000002, type 01000000 - size 28000
  Name: MMDevAPI.DLL
MZ at 74670000, prot 00000002, type 01000000 - size 32000
  Name: WINMM.dll
MZ at 746b0000, prot 00000002, type 01000000 - size 31000
  Name: TAPI32.dll
```

```
MZ at 749e0000, prot 00000002, type 01000000 - size 19e000
  Name: COMCTL32.dll
MZ at 74b80000, prot 00000002, type 01000000 - size 7000
  Name: AVRT.dll
MZ at 74ba0000, prot 00000002, type 01000000 - size 4a000
  Name: RASAPI32.dll
MZ at 74ce0000, prot 00000002, type 01000000 - size 3f000
  Name: UxTheme.dll
MZ at 74de0000, prot 00000002, type 01000000 - size 2d000
  Name: WINTRUST.dll
MZ at 74ea0000, prot 00000002, type 01000000 - size 14000
  Name: rasman.dll
MZ at 74f70000, prot 00000002, type 01000000 - size c000
  Name: rtutils.dll
MZ at 74f80000, prot 00000002, type 01000000 - size 5000
  Name: WSHTCPIP.dll
MZ at 74fb0000, prot 00000002, type 01000000 - size 21000
  Name: NTMARTA.dll
MZ at 75010000, prot 00000002, type 01000000 - size 3b000
  Name: RSAENH.dll
MZ at 75050000, prot 00000002, type 01000000 - size 5000
  Name: MSIMG32.dll
MZ at 75060000, prot 00000002, type 01000000 - size 15000
  Name: GPAPI.dll
MZ at 750a0000, prot 00000002, type 01000000 - size 46000
  Name: SCHANNEL.dll
MZ at 752b0000, prot 00000002, type 01000000 - size 3b000
  Name: MSWSOCK.dll
MZ at 75370000, prot 00000002, type 01000000 - size 45000
  Name: bcrypt.dll
MZ at 753f0000, prot 00000002, type 01000000 - size 5000
  Name: WSHIP6.dll
MZ at 75400000, prot 00000002, type 01000000 - size 8000
  Name: VERSION.dll
MZ at 75420000, prot 00000002, type 01000000 - size 7000
  Name: CREDSSP.dll
MZ at 75430000, prot 00000002, type 01000000 - size 35000
  Name: ncrypt.dll
MZ at 75480000, prot 00000002, type 01000000 - size 22000
  Name: dhcpcsvc6.DLL
MZ at 754b0000, prot 00000002, type 01000000 - size 7000
  Name: WINNSI.DLL
MZ at 754c0000, prot 00000002, type 01000000 - size 35000
  Name: dhcpcsvc.DLL
MZ at 75500000, prot 00000002, type 01000000 - size 19000
  Name: IPHLPAPI.DLL
MZ at 75590000, prot 00000002, type 01000000 - size 3a000
  Name: slc.dll
MZ at 755d0000, prot 00000002, type 01000000 - size f2000
  Name: CRYPT32.dll
MZ at 75740000, prot 00000002, type 01000000 - size 12000
  Name: MSASN1.dll
MZ at 75760000, prot 00000002, type 01000000 - size 11000
  Name: SAMLIB.dll
MZ at 75780000, prot 00000002, type 01000000 - size 76000
  Name: NETAPI32.dll
MZ at 75800000, prot 00000002, type 01000000 - size 2c000
  Name: DNSAPI.dll
MZ at 75a70000, prot 00000002, type 01000000 - size 5f000
  Name: sxs.dll
```

```
MZ at 75ad0000, prot 00000002, type 01000000 - size 2c000
  Name: apphelp.dll
MZ at 75b30000, prot 00000002, type 01000000 - size 14000
  Name: Secur32.dll
MZ at 75b50000, prot 00000002, type 01000000 - size 1e000
  Name: USERENV.dll
MZ at 75c90000, prot 00000002, type 01000000 - size 7000
  Name: PSAPI.DLL
MZ at 75ca0000, prot 00000002, type 01000000 - size c3000
  Name: RPCRT4.dll
MZ at 75d70000, prot 00000002, type 01000000 - size 73000
  Name: COMDLG32.dll
MZ at 75df0000, prot 00000002, type 01000000 - size 9000
  Name: LPK.dll
MZ at 75e00000, prot 00000002, type 01000000 - size dc000
  Name: KERNEL32.dll
MZ at 75ee0000, prot 00000002, type 01000000 - size aa000
  Name: msvcrt.dll
MZ at 75f90000, prot 00000002, type 01000000 - size 1e8000
  Name: iertutil.dll
MZ at 76180000, prot 00000002, type 01000000 - size 29000
  Name: imagehlp.dll
MZ at 761b0000, prot 00000002, type 01000000 - size 6000
  Name: NSI.dll
MZ at 761c0000, prot 00000002, type 01000000 - size 84000
  Name: CLBCatQ.DLL
MZ at 76250000, prot 00000002, type 01000000 - size 49000
  Name: WLDAP32.dll
MZ at 762a0000, prot 00000002, type 01000000 - size c6000
  Name: ADVAPI32.dll
MZ at 76370000, prot 00000002, type 01000000 - size 4b000
  Name: GDI32.dll
MZ at 763c0000, prot 00000002, type 01000000 - size 59000
  Name: SHLWAPI.dll
MZ at 76420000, prot 00000002, type 01000000 - size e6000
  Name: WININET.dll
MZ at 76510000, prot 00000002, type 01000000 - size b10000
  Name: SHELL32.dll
MZ at 77020000, prot 00000002, typc 01000000 - size 145000
  Name: ole32.dll
MZ at 77170000, prot 00000002, type 01000000 - size 7d000
  Name: USP10.dll
MZ at 771f0000, prot 00000002, type 01000000 - size 8d000
  Name: OLEAUT32.dll
MZ at 77280000, prot 00000002, type 01000000 - size 18a000
  Name: SETUPAPI.dll
MZ at 77410000, prot 00000002, type 01000000 - size 9d000
  Name: USER32.dll
MZ at 774b0000, prot 00000002, type 01000000 - size 133000
  Name: urlmon.dll
MZ at 775f0000, prot 00000002, type 01000000 - size 127000
  Name: ntdll.dll
MZ at 77720000, prot 00000002, type 01000000 - size 3000
  Name: Normaliz.dll
MZ at 77730000, prot 00000002, type 01000000 - size 2d000
  Name: WS2_32.dll
MZ at 77760000, prot 00000002, type 01000000 - size 1e000
  Name: IMM32.dll
MZ at 77780000, prot 00000002, type 01000000 - size c8000
  Name: MSCTF.dll
```

```
MZ at 7c340000, prot 00000002, type 01000000 - size 56000
  Name: MSVCR71.dll
```

The check that module start address:

```
0:005> !address 10000000
Usage:                  <unclassified>
Allocation Base:        10000000
Base Address:           10000000
End Address:            10001000
Region Size:            00001000
Type:                   00020000 MEM_PRIVATE
State:                  00001000 MEM_COMMIT
Protect:                00000004 PAGE_READWRITE
```

Finally if we search the first found module address range for ASCII strings we find some interesting fragments:

```
0:005> s-sa 00040000 L1d000
0004004d  "!This program cannot be run in D"
0004006d  "OS mode."
00040081  "3y@"
000400b8  "Rich"
000401d0  ".text"
000401f7  "`.rdata"
0004021f  "@.data"
00040248  ".reloc"
[...]
00054010  "READY"
00054018  "GET /stat?uptime=%d&downlink=%d&"
00054038  "uplink=%d&id=%s&statpass=%s&comm"
00054058  "ent=%s HTTP/1.0"
000540ac  "%s%s%s"
000540d8  "ftp://%s:%s@%s:%d"
000540fc  "Accept-Encoding:"
00054118  "Accept-Encoding:"
00054130  "0123456789ABCDEF"
00054144  "://"
00054160  "POST %s HTTP/1.0"
00054172  "Host: %s"
0005417c  "User-Agent: %s"
0005418c  "Accept: text/html"
0005419f  "Connection: Close"
000541b2  "Content-Type: application/x-www-"
000541d2  "form-urlencoded"
000541e3  "Content-Length: %d"
000541fc  "id="
00054208  "POST %s HTTP/1.1"
0005421a  "Host: %s"
00054224  "User-Agent: %s"
00054234  "Accept: text/html"
00054247  "Connection: Close"
0005425a  "Content-Type: application/x-www-"
0005427a  "form-urlencoded"
0005428b  "Content-Length: %d"
000542a4  "id=%s&base="
000542b8  "id=%s&brw=%d&type=%d&data="
000542d8  "POST %s HTTP/1.1"
000542ea  "Host: %s"
000542f4  "User-Agent: %s"
```

```
00054304    "Accept: text/html"
00054317    "Connection: Close"
0005432a    "Content-Type: application/x-www-"
0005434a    "form-urlencoded"
0005435b    "Content-Length: %d"
00054378    "id=%s&os=%s&plist="
00054390    "POST %s HTTP/1.1"
000543a2    "Host: %s"
000543ac    "User-Agent: %s"
000543bc    "Accept: text/html"
000543cf    "Connection: Close"
000543e2    "Content-Type: application/x-www-"
00054402    "form-urlencoded"
00054413    "Content-Length: %d"
00054430    "id=%s&data=%s"
00054440    "POST %s HTTP/1.1"
00054452    "Host: %s"
0005445c    "User-Agent: %s"
0005446c    "Accept: text/html"
0005447f    "Connection: Close"
00054492    "Content-Type: application/x-www-"
000544b2    "form-urlencoded"
000544c3    "Content-Length: %d"
000544e0    "GET %s HTTP/1.0"
000544f1    "Host: %s"
000544fb    "User-Agent: %s"
0005450b    "Connection: close"
00054528    "POST /get/scr.html HTTP/1.0"
00054545    "Host: %s"
0005454f    "User-Agent: %s"
0005455f    "Connection: close"
00054572    "Content-Length: %d"
00054586    "Content-Type: multipart/form-dat"
000545a6    "a; boundary=--------------------"
000545c6    "-------%d"
000545d4    "--------------------------%d"
000545f8    "%sContent-Disposition: form-data"
00054618    "; name="id""
00054630    "%sContent-Disposition: form-data"
00054650    "; name="screen"; filename="%d""
00054670    "Content-Type: application/octet-"
00054690    "stream"
000546a0    "%s(%d) : %s"
000546ac    "%s failed with error %d: %s"
000546c8    "%02X"
000546d8    "BlackwoodPRO"
000546e8    "FinamDirect"
000546f4    "GrayBox"
000546fc    "MbtPRO"
00054704    "Laser"
0005470c    "LightSpeed"
00054718    "LTGroup"
00054720    "Mbt"
00054724    "ScotTrader"
00054730    "SaxoTrader"
00054740    "Program:    %s"
0005474f    "Username:   %s"
0005475e    "Password:   %s"
0005476d    "AccountNO: %s"
0005477c    "Server:     %s"
```

```
00054790   "%s %s"
0005479c   "PROCESSOR_IDENTIFIER"
000547b8   "%02X"
000547c8   "%02X"
00055048   "naaac`+fjh"
[...]
```

Further Reading

Victimology

- Criminology: The Basics by S. Walklate
- The Praeger Handbook of Victimology by J. K. Wilson

Software Victimology

Software Diagnostics

- Software Diagnostics Institute
- Memory Dump Analysis Anthology: Volumes 1, 2, 3, 4, 5, 6, 7, …
  Volume 6 to be released in July / Volume 7 is planned for the end of 2012
- Software Trace and Memory Dump Analysis: Patterns, Tools, Processes and Best Practices
- Introduction to Pattern-Driven Software Problem Solving
- Fundamentals of Complete Crash and Hang Memory Dump Analysis
- Introduction to Pattern-Driven Software Diagnostics

Now some references. There is one short book on Criminology which covers Victimology as well. The other one, a handbook, has lots of useful conceptual articles related to human victimology. I also included links to relevant presentations and books from software diagnostics here that cover patterns.

Software Victimology:
http://www.dumpanalysis.org/blog/index.php/category/victimware/

Software Diagnostics Institute:
http://www.dumpanalysis.org/

Memory Dump Analysis Anthology:
http://www.patterndiagnostics.com/ultimate-memory-analysis-reference/

Software Trace and Memory Dump Analysis: Patterns, Tools, Processes and Best Practices:
http://www.patterndiagnostics.com/STMDA-materials/

Introduction to Pattern-Driven Software Problem Solving:
http://www.patterndiagnostics.com/PDSPSI-materials/

Fundamentals of Complete Crash and Hang Memory Dump Analysis:
http://www.patterndiagnostics.com/FCMDA-materials-Rev2/

Introduction to Pattern-Driven Software Diagnostics:
http://www.patterndiagnostics.com/Introduction-Software-Diagnostics-materials/

Philosophy of Software Diagnostics

Introduction

Part 1, Version 1.0

Dmitry Vostokov
Software Diagnostics Services

Philosophy of Software Diagnostics

Introduction, Part I

Version 1.0

Dmitry Vostokov
Software Diagnostics Services

Hello Everyone, my name is Dmitry Vostokov and today I make the first step towards a philosophy of software diagnostics. I decided to keep this presentation as short and simple as possible without using specialized philosophical jargon. If anything needs to be added or modified in the future I create another version of it. This is also the part one of the introduction because as a practicing software diagnostician I didn't have much time to process and include all material that I planned initially. So I promise to deliver the subsequent parts later. In this part we cover mostly phenomenological and hermeneutical approaches to software diagnostics and leave analytical approaches for the second part.

If want to be the best software diagnostician you need to be a philosopher.

After Galen's thoughts on medicine

Let me prefix the presentation by extending thoughts of the great Roman physician and philosopher Galen to software diagnostics.

These prerequisites are very simple and I suppose you all, like me, enjoy diagnosing software problems, troubleshooting and debugging. Also philosophical attitude presupposes interest in deep meta-questions. In our interpretation of meta-, "What is a problem here?" is a question, but "What is a problem?" is a meta-question.

Our goal is to synthesize the philosophy of software diagnostics from the software diagnostics practice itself.

Software Diagnostics

A discipline studying abnormal software structure and behavior in software execution artifacts (such as memory dumps, software and network traces and logs) using pattern-oriented analysis methodologies.

© 2013 Software Diagnostics Services

Before we start with philosophy I would like to remind you about a definition of software diagnostics that we put forward in our previous webinars. Notice the appearance of a word "pattern" here. So what is a pattern then?

Diagnostics Pattern

A common recurrent identifiable problem together with a set of recommendations and possible solutions to apply in a specific context.

The definition of a diagnostics pattern is more general because it applies not only to software artifacts but to hardware and software diagnostics itself and if you'd like it can be applied to general diagnostics as well. Notice also the appearance of a word "problem" here. Obviously, in the previous definition the so called "abnormal software structure and behavior" is also some kind of a problem. Therefore, to understand a diagnostics thought process and diagnostics patterns we need to ask a further question.

The First Question

What is a Problem?

There are many definitions of a problem especially from the problem solving perspective. But a diagnosis is not a problem solving and before doing correct diagnosis we must be sure that we have a right problem but to find out whether we have a right problem we need to perform a correct diagnosis. Vicious circle. So we need a very simple definition of the problem that doesn't involve a diagnosis. We consider problems from human computer interaction first because such interactions are everywhere and involve everyone including the vast industry of software support. In order to find out the best definition we opened **Historical Thesaurus of the Oxford English Dictionary, 2 volume set.**

Problem

- **Difficulty** – problem 1641 business 1843 (colloq.) core c1460-1652 prob 1934 (colloq.) hang-up 1959 (slang) problem 1874 sub-problem 1907 pseudo-problem 1911
- **Mathematics** – prob 1864
- **Materials of topic of debate / discussion** – problem 1529 – 1646 (question, thesis, argument, issue, consultation, debating point)
- **Enquiry, questioning** – problem 1594 good question 1918

Historical thesaurus shows the concept variations in time and adds an additional dimension to the meaning and can be a source of new ideas. On the slide I put an excerpt from different domains. The main meaning there is "Difficulty". We have a problem when we have difficulty while interacting with software. We consider enquiry, questioning and discussion later. With such a definition if we have a memory leak but if it is going unnoticeable we don't have a problem. Notice the abbreviation of problem as **prob** and use it as such in mathematics. To differentiate our problem from any other definition we came up with a new word for it.

Prob-lem(ma)

A prob-lemma is a pair:

- ⊙ An issue
- ⊙ ~Understanding of an issue

Проблема (Problema, in Russian)

We call it **prob-lemma**. What is a **lemma** part? In mathematics, **lemma** is defined as a proven proposition which is used as a stepping stone to a larger result. In our context it is a tentative proposition about a probable problem. It is often a case that a problem disappears before diagnostics starts or is relative or stems from software user misunderstanding. We define **prob-lemma** as a pair: it is an issue for a software user (difficulty) but an understanding of it is absent or vague or incomplete. Tilde here means a negation, a negation of understanding of the issue. The first time I see my Russian roots help me in problem solving, in problem solving the problem of the problem.

Sometimes we are lucky and understand a problem but most of the time we don't have its understanding.

The key to understanding is a projection of a problem to patterns. But not all patterns are good for understanding. We need ...

Patterns

Pattern-in-artefact

... patterns in artefacts. By an artefact we mean a memory dump, or live memory (which is a sort of a memory dump), software traces and logs whose messages can be considered as fragments of memory similar to memory dumps. And so we come to a second concept called ...

Da-sign

- A pattern in the artefact for an issue that has a concern for us
- **Understanding** of an issue and a pattern

Da- in **da-sign** means a dump artefact and a **-sign** part means just a sign, a pattern. If we able to get a collection of **da-signs** for a **prob-lemma** we get full understanding of an original problem. You may have noticed that **Da-sign** is similar to *Da-sein* introduced in influential "Being and Time" philosophical log from Martin Heidegger, a German philosopher. It means "being there", a peculiar human being whose being is an issue for it and it has an understanding of it. In our context **da-sign** means "a sign there, in a dump", a peculiar software structure and behaviour sign that we are aware of and have an understanding of it. Note a word "understanding here". We now come to the question of understanding. But before we consider understanding we would like to note that **da-signs** are not floating in isolation. We need a meaning-structure for them.

CARE

- Da-sign as a meaning-pattern

- Underlying meaning-structure for da-signs

We call it CARE. Originally it meant crash analysis report environment or computer analysis report analysis. **Da-signs** are themselves meaning-patterns and CARE is their underlying meaning-structure. Now we continue with the question of Understanding.

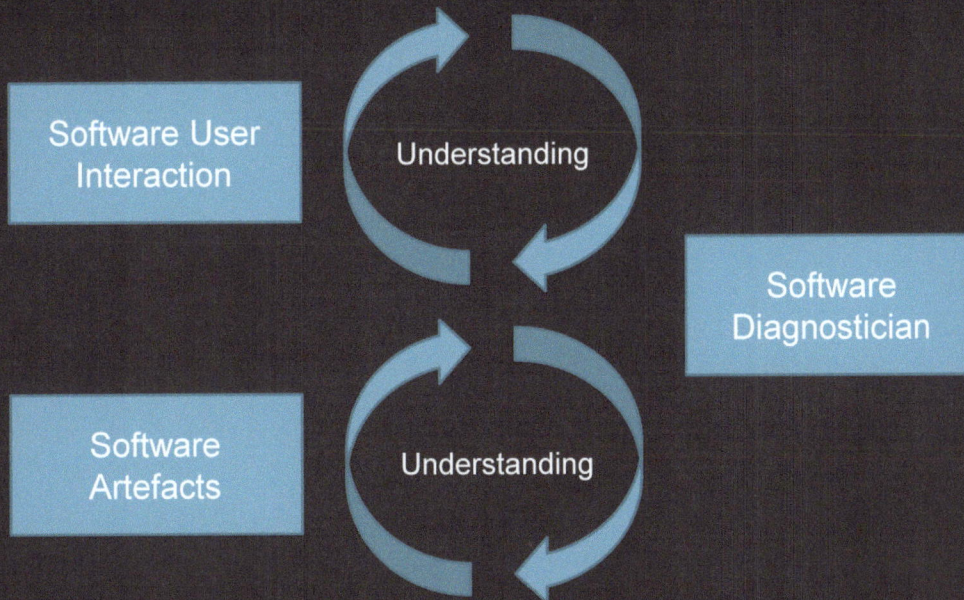

Hermeneutics

Software User Interaction

Understanding

Software Diagnostician

Software Artefacts

Understanding

Software Diagnostics is a practice and based on a dialog, understanding and interpretive interactions between a software diagnostician and a software user. Such meetings and dialogs are even more important in the case of remote interactions.

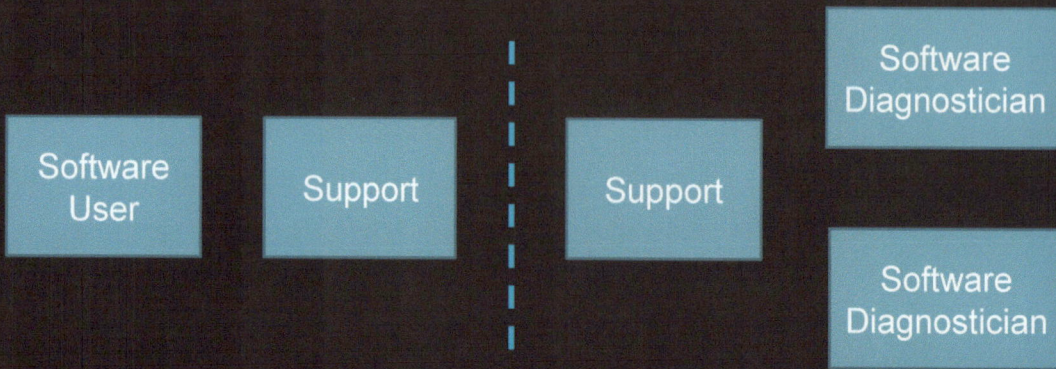

Remote Interaction

Software User

Support

Support

Software Diagnostician

Software Diagnostician

© 2013 Software Diagnostics Services

Here on this diagram I depicted possible interaction parties. For large software vendors and their customers there can be even more intermediate interactions until finally an artefact is opened in some analysis tool. There can be several software diagnostics practitioners such as technical support engineers, escalation, technical relationship managers, maintenance software engineers and software product developers.

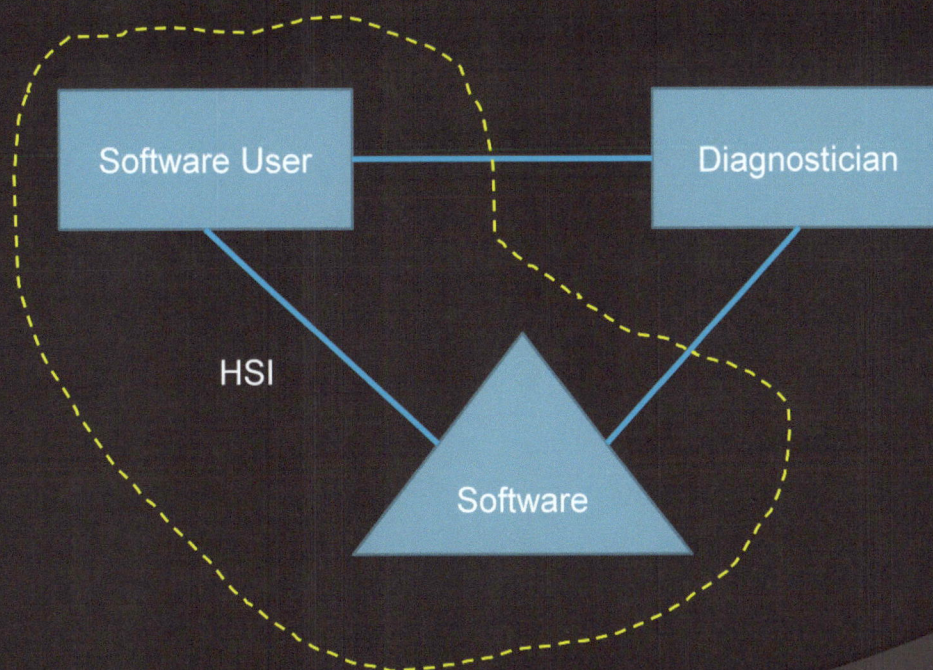

Software diagnostics as a practice involves humans using software. Therefore it is beneficial to consider both software users and software when thinking about software diagnostics.

Understanding Patterns

- Existing patterns

- Excavating new patterns

- Better understanding of software

Working with patterns of defects makes one understanding of software better. When a breakdown of a computation happens we notice a pattern of software structure and behaviour and add it to a catalogue.

Sources of Interpretation

- Problem descriptions

- Human-software interaction

- Interaction itself

- Artefacts

Understanding goes with interpretation. Due to various omissions, insufficient and incomplete interaction documentation it is always possible to interpret or misinterpret problem differently due to shifting requirements, different normative and political considerations. There can be different sources for interpretation.

Phenomenology

Various phenomena (patterns) in:

HCI

Life-world

Computer-world

Artefacts

I became interested in phenomenology last year. In the context of software diagnostics it is about the meaning and structure of everyday software diagnostics activities.

Why Phenomenology?

- Involves human side
- About meaning and understanding
- Includes feeling and mood

The best of Husserl and Heidegger

Additional feature of phenomenology that can be useful for holistic philosophy of software diagnostics is its inclusion of the human side.

Patterns as Phenomena

- Meaning-structures in meaningful world of experience

- Common meaning-structure

- Leaving Human-Software dichotomy outside: patterns of phenomena

I borrowed meaning-structure and meaning-pattern words from the book on phenomenology and hermeneutics of medicine I reference at the end of this presentation.

Software Phenomenology

- Only experience
- Bracketing implementation [code]
- "Free fantasy variation" (Husserl)

Free fantasy investigation

(software narratology)

- Pattern discourse
- Common meaning-structure in Computer-world

Here I highlighted some features of software diagnostics phenomenology.

Hermeneutics

- Meeting and dialog narratives

- Software problem narratives

- Software execution narratives

- Software trace and log patterns

Hermeneutics is about interpretation and understanding. It involves the analysis of narrative stories and in software diagnostics there are different types of them to consider.

Usually phenomenology goes with hermeneutics. Typical example here is problem description narratives that can be interpreted and understood with the help of problem description patterns.

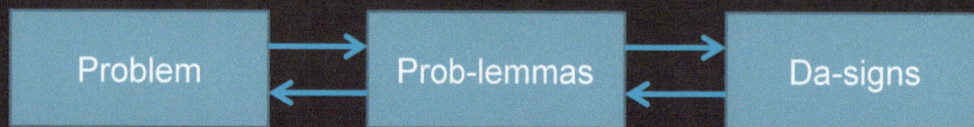

Software diagnosis provides possible explanation for the problem. After finding **da-signs** we refine our **prob-lemmas** and provide explanation, recommendation and possible solutions for the original software problem.

© 2013 Software Diagnostics Services

As a conclusion you see that software diagnostics is mainly human-assisted. What about computer assistance?

Computer Assistance

- (Logic, Language, Software) ➡ Medicine

- (Logic, Language, Software) ➡ Software

The medical diagnostics was used as a systemic prototype for analogy and metaphors. However, there is crucial difference here. In medicine the logic of software is imposed on medical diagnostics (the so called analytical approach) but in software diagnostics software is inherent. So we come to the analytical philosophy of software diagnostics.

Analytical Philosophy

Software as a Logico-Linguistic Machine

We leave it for the second part we plan to introduce in a few months.

Abductive Diagnostics

1. Fact: B
2. "If A then B" explains B
3. Root cause A is probable

Originally we planned this webinar to be focused on abduction only. What is abductive reasoning you see from the example here. Abduction is very common in medical diagnostics and law, for example. However, we found that software diagnostics was missing philosophical foundations and prepared this webinar instead. We promise to cover abductive logic and its relation to philosophy of software diagnostics in the next part.

Further Reading

Philosophy

- *"Martin Heidegger: The Possibility of A Russian Philosophy"* by A. Dugin (in Russian language)
- *"Introduction to Metaphysics"* by Martin Heidegger
- *"Being and Time"* by Martin Heidegger (blue book)
- *"Heidegger: A Guide for the Perplexed"* by David Cerbone
- *"The Hermeneutics of Medicine and the Phenomenology of Health: Steps Towards a Philosophy of Medical Practice"* by Fredrik Svenaeus

Pattern-Oriented Software Diagnostics

- Software Diagnostics Institute
- Memory Dump Analysis Anthology: Volumes 1, 2, 3, 4, 5, 6, 7, 8, ...
  Volume 7 is in preparation (May-June, 2013)
- Introduction to Pattern-Driven Software Diagnostics
- Introduction to Systemic Software Diagnostics
- Introduction to Pattern-Based Software Diagnostics
- Introduction to Software Narratology

Here are some books I recommend to read. The first one (unfortunately is only available for Russian readers) was very influential for me to see the possibility of software diagnostics philosophy. The second one, an introduction to metaphysics, prompted me to delve deeper into a definition of a **problem** word. The next two books: *Being and Time* and its interpretation guide gave me ideas for **da-sign**. And finally, the book about hermeneutics and phenomenology gave me ideas on meaning-structures and meaning-patterns. The second section lists resources for pattern-oriented software diagnostics.

Software Diagnostics Institute:

http://www.dumpanalysis.org

Memory Dump Analysis Anthology volumes:

http://www.patterndiagnostics.com/ultimate-memory-analysis-reference

Introduction to Pattern-Driven Software Diagnostics:

http://www.patterndiagnostics.com/Introduction-Software-Diagnostics-materials

Introduction to Systemic Software Diagnostics:

http://www.patterndiagnostics.com/systemic-diagnostics-materials

Introduction to Pattern-Based Software Diagnostics:

http://www.patterndiagnostics.com/pattern-based-diagnostics-materials

Introduction to Software Narratology:

http://www.patterndiagnostics.com/Introduction-Software-Narratology-materials

Software and Time

Your PC ran into a problem that it couldn't handle, and now it needs to restart.

You can search for the error online: CRITICAL_OBJECT_TERMINATION

BEING AND TIME

Martin Heidegger

© 2013 Software Diagnostics Services

For those who consider that life is similar to software I provide this pictorial analogy. Philosophy of Heidegger incorporates death as an inescapable part of human being and we also consider "blue screens of death" as an inescapable part of software. Note that the philosophy of Heidegger is considered as a philosophy of death and a philosophy of a new beginning.

Malware
Narratives
Introduction

Version 1.0

Dmitry Vostokov
Software Diagnostics Services

Published by OpenTask, Republic of Ireland

OpenTask books and magazines are available through booksellers and distributors worldwide. For further information or comments send requests to press@opentask.com.

A CIP catalogue record for this book is available from the British Library.

ISBN-l3: 978-1-908043-48-1 (Paperback)

First printing, 2013

Hello Everyone, my name is Dmitry Vostokov and I introduce today a software narratological approach to malware analysis of software traces and logs. I decided to keep this presentation short and as simple as possible. If anything needs to be added or modified in the future I create another version of it.

Facebook:
http://www.facebook.com/SoftwareDiagnosticsServices

Linkedin:
http://www.linkedin.com/company/software-diagnostics-services

Twitter:
http://twitter.com/DumpAnalysis

Prerequisites

Interest in software diagnostics and malware analysis

These prerequisites are very simple and I suppose you all like me enjoy diagnosing malware and often going side-by-side corresponding software problems.

Why?

- ◉ Communication language

- ◉ Malware diagnostics as software diagnostics

- ◉ Big DA+TA (Dump Artifacts + Trace Artifacts)

Why we advocate a different approach to traditional log analysis? First, we need a unified communication language in the context of general software diagnostics, and second, an approach to tackle big DA+TA that is in our context means memory dump and trace artifacts. The proliferation of mobile technologies might seem making memory dump analysis redundant but the size of memory is ever increasing for mobile and embedded devices and software traces ad logs are just a form of memory dumps.

Software Diagnostics

A discipline studying abnormal software structure and behavior in software execution artifacts (such as memory dumps, software and network traces and logs) using pattern-driven, systemic and pattern-based analysis methodologies.

© 2013 Software Diagnostics Services

First, I would like to remind you a definition of software diagnostics we put forward in one of our previous webinars. We also use words such as "trace" and "log" interchangeably. So you see that malware detection and associated software behavior fall under the definition of software diagnostics.

Pattern-driven:
http://www.patterndiagnostics.com/Introduction-Software-Diagnostics-materials

Systemic:
http://www.patterndiagnostics.com/systemic-diagnostics-materials

Pattern-based:
http://www.dumpanalysis.org/pattern-based-software-diagnostics

Diagnostics Pattern

A common recurrent identifiable problem together with a set of recommendations and possible solutions to apply in a specific context.

Next we would like to mention a definition of a software diagnostics pattern. There are some differences with a usual definition of a pattern from software construction such as architectural and design patterns. The difference is that often upon a diagnostic encounter we provide recommendations and possible solutions instead of just problem solutions. Recommendations may include immediate actions, for example, upon the detection of suspicious activity.

Pattern Orientation

Pattern-driven

- ◉ Finding patterns in software artefacts
- ◉ Using checklists and pattern catalogs

Pattern-based

- ◉ Pattern catalog evolution
- ◉ Catalog packaging and delivery

So you see that software diagnostics is about patterns and pattern recognition. Let's say it is pattern-oriented and includes pattern-based and pattern-driven parts. Pattern-driven is about diagnostics process and pattern-based is about pattern life cycle. We first start with the pattern-driven part first.

Catalog Classification

- By abstraction

Meta-patterns

- By artifact type

Software Log*   Memory Dump   Network Trace*

- By story type

Problem Description   Software Disruption   UI Problem

- By intention

Malware

In pattern-driven analysis we use pattern catalogs. Catalogs can be classified by abstraction, for example, as software diagnostics meta-patterns which are patterns of software diagnostics itself, by the type of software execution artifacts, such as software traces and logs, memory dumps and network traces, by story type, such as by problem descriptions, by software disruptions, and by user interface problems. Also we can separate patterns by intention such as malware (with unintentional patterns, the rest, all grouped as Victimware). In this presentation we only consider software logs and network traces.

Meta-patterns:
http://www.dumpanalysis.org/blog/index.php/2012/06/09/patterns-of-software-diagnostics-part-1/

Software Log:
http://www.dumpanalysis.org/blog/index.php/trace-analysis-patterns/

Memory Dump:
http://www.dumpanalysis.org/blog/index.php/crash-dump-analysis-patterns/

Network Trace:
http://www.dumpanalysis.org/blog/index.php/2012/07/19/network-trace-analysis-patterns-part-1/

Problem Description:
http://www.dumpanalysis.org/blog/index.php/2012/03/11/software-problem-description-patterns-part-1/

Software Disruption:
http://www.dumpanalysis.org/blog/index.php/2013/01/12/software-disruption-patterns-part-1/

UI Problem:
http://www.dumpanalysis.org/blog/index.php/user-interface-problem-analysis-patterns/

Malware:
http://www.dumpanalysis.org/blog/index.php/malware-analysis-patterns/

Malware

Software that uses planned alteration of structure and behavior of software to serve malicious purposes.

Because our presentation is related to malware we provide its definition: software that uses planned alteration of structure and behavior of software to serve malicious purposes. Notice the recursive character of that definition that includes self-modifying malware and also rootkits where a malicious purpose is to conceal.

Memory Analysis Patterns

Software Diagnostics

Memory Dump
Analysis
Patterns

Malware
Analysis
Patterns

Before we proceed to software traces and logs I would like to say a few words about memory and memory dumps. Some time ago we created a separate malware pattern catalog for memory analysis. Due to intentional nature of malware there is only a partial overlap of them, for example, **Out-of-Module Pointer** (a pointer in a structure is considered malicious if it points outside the module code range) is considered to be malware specific.

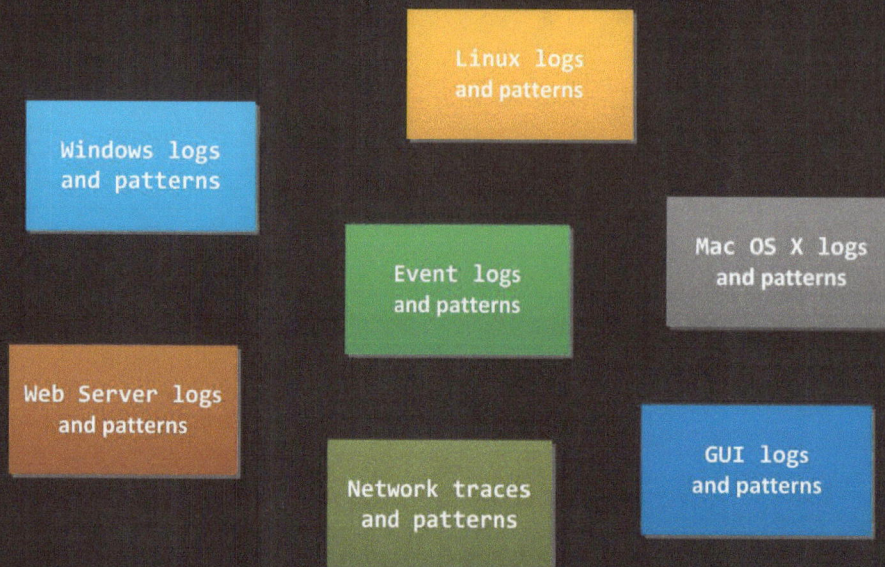

Traces and Logs

Linux logs and patterns

Windows logs and patterns

Event logs and patterns

Mac OS X logs and patterns

Web Server logs and patterns

Network traces and patterns

GUI logs and patterns

© 2013 Software Diagnostics Services

In addition to live memory and memory snapshot artifacts software diagnostics also analyses various software traces and logs. There are so many of them with different formats, OS and product specific information.

Trace and Log Patterns

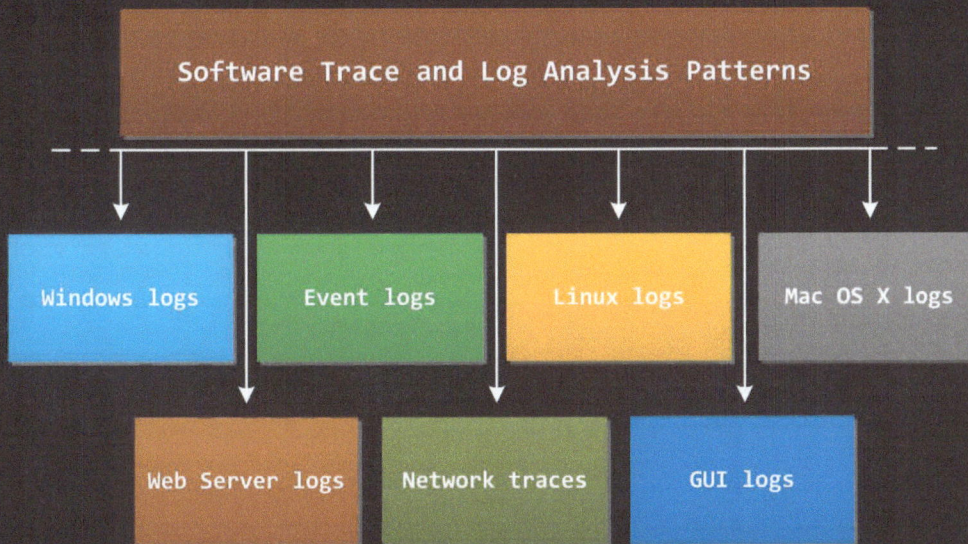

Software Trace and Log Analysis Patterns

- Windows logs
- Event logs
- Linux logs
- Mac OS X logs
- Web Server logs
- Network traces
- GUI logs

© 2013 Software Diagnostics Services

A unifying approach was needed for a pattern catalog. The needed solution would use the common structure of all these logs and associated patterns.

Software Narrative

A temporal sequence of events related to software execution.

We, therefore, considered using narratology, the discipline that studies various narrative forms such as stories, novels, movies because all these logs have the same unified narrative structure such as events ordered by time.

Narrative Taxonomy

- Incident stories
- Software traces and logs
- Malware analysis stories

There are several types of narrative related to malware analysis. In this presentation we only limit ourselves to software traces and logs as stories of software execution and communication.

Malware Narrative Patterns

Software Trace and Log Analysis Patterns

Malware Narrative Patterns

Software Diagnostics

© 2013 Software Diagnostics Services

By malware narrative patterns we consider a subset of software trace and log analysis patterns because the same logs can also be used for the analysis of abnormal software behaviour, troubleshooting and debugging, and they all have the same underlying narratological structure.

Software Log

- A sequence of formatted messages
- Arranged by time
- A narrative story

What is a software trace or log actually? For our purposes it is just a sequence of formatted messages sent from running software, for example, an event log or intercepted and formatted API requests such as a log from Process Monitor tool or even a network trace. They are usually arranged by time and can be considered as a software narrative story.

Minimal Log Graphs

```
No Module  PID  TID  Date       Time          Message
------------------------------------------------------------
1  ModuleA 4280 1736 5/28/2012 08:53:50.496 Trace message 1
2  ModuleB 6212 6216 5/28/2012 08:53:52.876 Trace message 2
[...]
```

© 2013 Software Diagnostics Services

In order to illustrate log analysis patterns graphically we use the simplified abstracted pictorial representation of a typical software log. It has all essential features such as message number, time, PID, TID, and message text itself.

A few words about logs, checklists, and patterns. Software log analysis is usually an analysis of a text for the presence of patterns. Here checklists can be very useful.

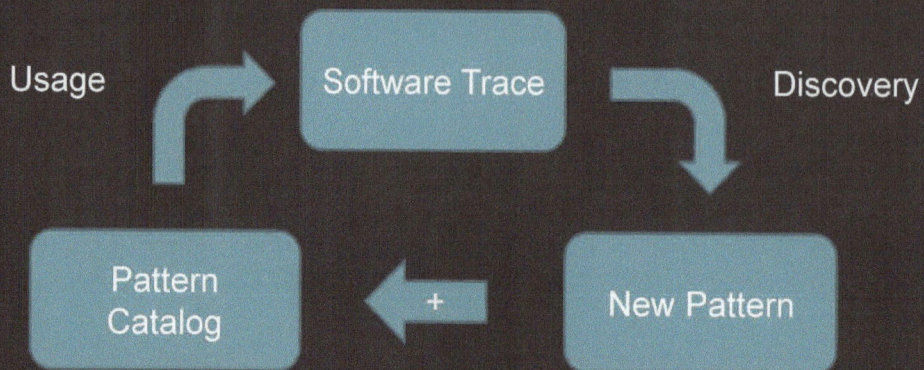

Pattern catalogs are rarely fixed. New patterns are constantly discerned or refined. For example, while preparing for this webinar I found yet another missing pattern and added it to the trace analysis pattern catalog.

Pattern Classification

- ⊙ Vocabulary
- ⊙ Error
- ⊙ Trace as a Whole
- ⊙ Large Scale
- ⊙ Activity
- ⊙ Message
- ⊙ Block
- ⊙ Trace Set

Recently all software trace and log analysis patterns (which are now numbered almost 70 at the time of this writing) were classified into several categories. Vocabulary category consists of patterns related to problem description. Error category covers general error distribution patterns. This classification also considers traces as wholes, their large scale structure, activity patterns, patterns related to individual trace message structure, patterns related to collection of messages (the so called blocks) and finally patterns related to several traces and logs as a collection of artifacts from software incident. Because malware detection and analysis is only a part of general software diagnostics we selected only a few patterns from these categories as relevant. Of course, all this selection will be revised in the future version of this classification.

Reference and Course

- ◉ Free catalog

  Software Log Analysis Patterns

- ◉ Free reference graphical slides

  Accelerated-Windows-Software-Trace-Analysis-Public.pdf

- ◉ Training course*

  Accelerated Windows Software Trace Analysis

  * Available as a full color paperback book, PDF book, on SkillSoft Books 24x7. Recording is available for all book formats

Most of patterns are very intuitive if you analyse logs and traces. Here I provided a few links and after you download a presentation you can follow them. Although most pattern examples are for Windows platform they are really platform and product independent.

Software Log Analysis Patterns[1]:
http://www.dumpanalysis.org/blog/index.php/trace-analysis-patterns/

Free reference graphical slides:
http://www.patterndiagnostics.com/Training/Accelerated-Windows-Software-Trace-Analysis-Public.pdf

Training course:
http://www.patterndiagnostics.com/accelerated-software-trace-analysis

---

[1] No longer free, please contact Software Diagnostics Services at www.PatternDiagnostics.com

Vocabulary Patterns

- Basic Facts*
- Vocabulary Index

* patterns marked with yellow color are most likely to be useful for malware detection and analysis

The first block of patterns are vocabulary patterns related to an incident description from a user point of view. A typical log is a detailed software narrative that might include lots of irrelevant information with useful messages like needles in a haystack. However, it is usually accompanied by an incident description that lists essential facts. Therefore the first task of any log analysis is to check the presence of **Basic Facts** (or it is usually called *Supporting Materials*) in the log. If they are not visible or do not correspond then the trace was possibly not recorded during the incident or was taken from a different computer or under different conditions.

Error Patterns

- Error Message
- Exception Stack Trace
- False Positive Error
- Periodic Error
- Error Distribution

The next block are error patterns related to error and failure messages either explicitly stating that there is an error or doing that indirectly via error code, abnormal function return value or NT status values in failure range. These patterns may be relevant when some malware causes some malfunction (the so called victimware) or itself experiences abnormal behavior. We do not cover them here.

Trace as a Whole

- Partition
- Circular Trace
- Message Density
- Message Current
- Trace Acceleration
- No Trace Metafile
- Empty Trace
- Missing Module
- Guest Module

- Truncated Trace
- Visibility Limit
- Sparse Trace

The third block of patterns contains patterns related to software trace or log as a whole. We ignore trace message contents and treat all messages statistically. Here we see only one pattern relevant to malware analysis specifically and it is called **Guest Module**.

Guest Module

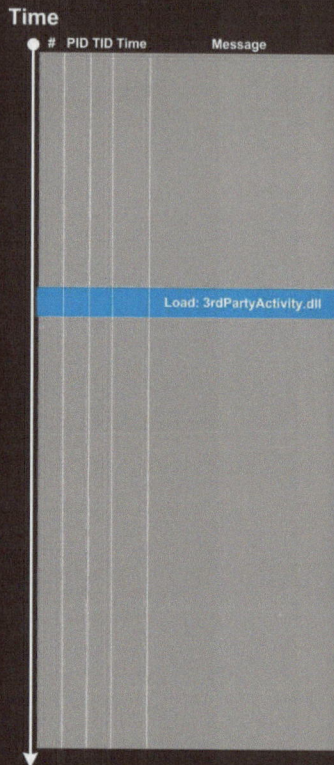

Time

#	PID TID Time	Message
		Load: 3rdPartyActivity.dll

© 2013 Software Diagnostics Services

Often, when comparing normal, expected and suspicious traces we can get clues by looking at module load events. For example, when we see an unexpected module load event in our suspicious trace this may prompt us to investigate it further.

Large Scale Patterns

- Characteristic Block
- Background Modules
- Foreground Modules
- Layered Periodization
- Focus of Tracing
- Event Sequence Order
- Trace Frames

The fourth block consists of large scale log patterns. They are about the coarse grain structure of software traces and logs where the division unit is often a module or some high level functionality. Here we would like to highlight 3 patterns that make sense for malware detection and analysis: **Characteristic Block**, **Foreground Modules**, and **Focus of Tracing**.

Characteristic Block

Textual representations can also be viewed a from bird's eye perspective. Irregularities in formatting make it easier to see coarse blocked structure of a software trace or log.

Foreground Modules

Log and trace viewers such as Process Monitor and network analysis tools can filter out (or exclude) background component messages and present only foreground modules (that we call **module** or **component foregrounding**). Here background modules can be considered as noise to filter out. Of course, this process is iterative and parts of what once was foreground become background and candidates for further filtering.

Focus of Tracing

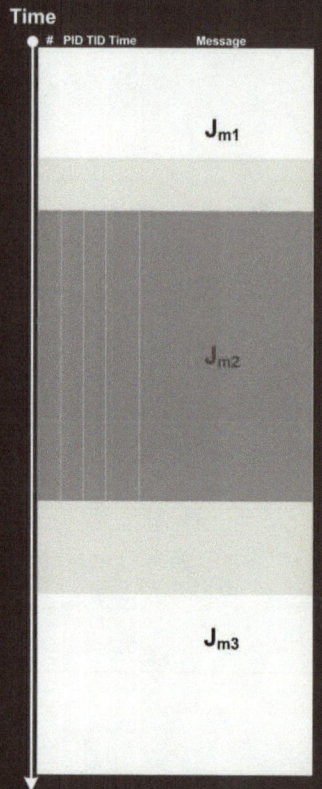

Activity regions: J_{m1}, J_{m2}, J_{m3}

© 2013 Software Diagnostics Services

A software trace or log consists of the so called **Activity Regions** with syntactical and visual aspects of log analysis whereas **Focus of Tracing** brings attention to changing semantics of log message flow. Here is a graphical illustration of this pattern where tracing focus region spans 3 regions of activity.

Activity Patterns

- Thread of Activity
- Adjoint Thread of Activity
- No Activity
- Activity Region
- Discontinuity
- Time Delta
- Glued Activity
- Break-in Activity
- Resume Activity
- Data Flow

The fifth block of patterns is related to various software activities we see in logs and traces. Most of them involve time dependency.

Thread of Activity

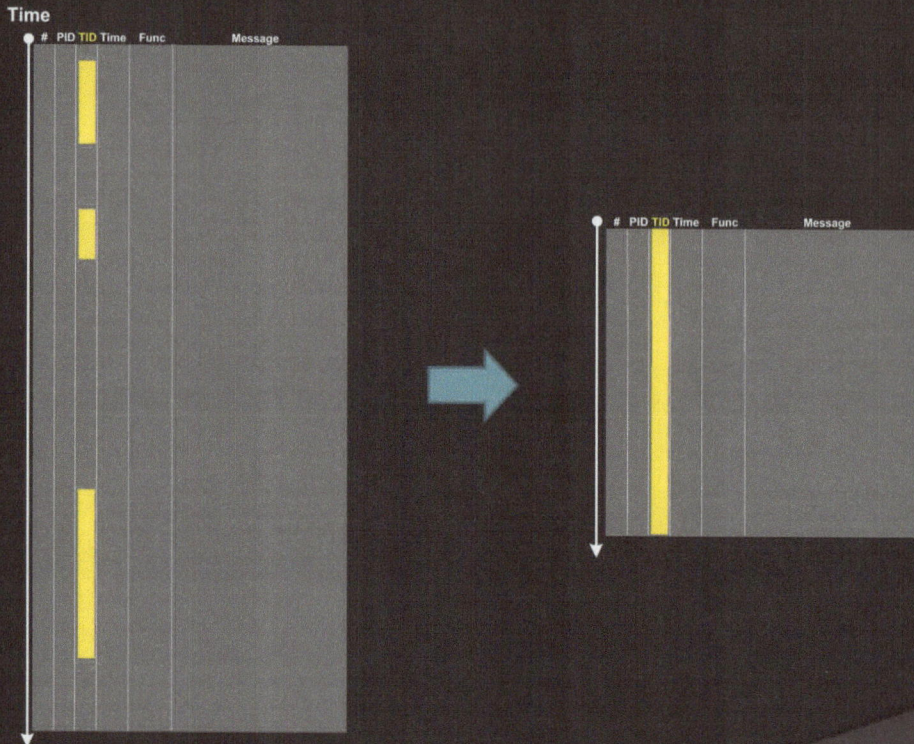

© 2013 Software Diagnostics Services

This pattern means trace messages associated with particular TID. When we see a suspicious message we select its current thread and investigate what happened in this process and thread before.

Adjoint Thread of Activity

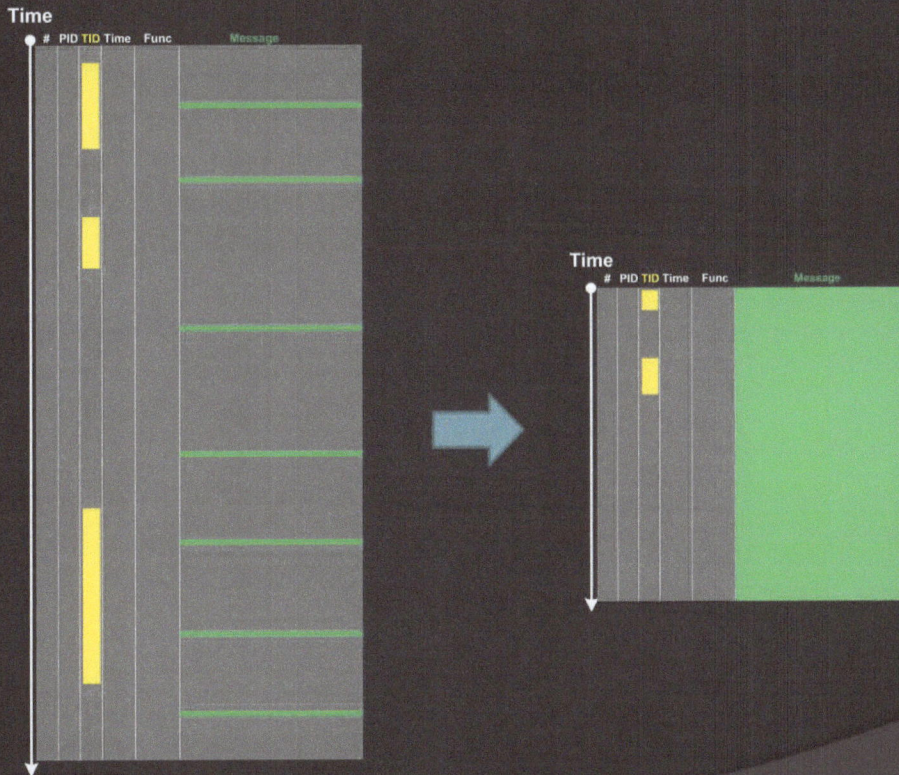

© 2013 Software Diagnostics Services

Adjoint Thread is an extension of **Thread of Activity** pattern. On the picture we see a log message stream where some messages are coming from specific TID shown in yellow color. Suppose we are interested in some specific network operation or registry or file activity or process name. It is possible to filter such messages and form an adjoint thread of activity for further pattern analysis.

Activity Region

Message current : $J_{m2} > \max(J_{m1}, J_{m3})$

© 2013 Software Diagnostics Services

Basically it is a region of log message stream messages related semantically or syntactically. Of course it is all relative and dependent on analysis goals. For example, when looking at long traces with millions of messages we can see regions of activity where **Message Current** (J_m, msg/s) is much higher than in surrounding temporal regions. Another example is sudden network activity region.

Glued Activity

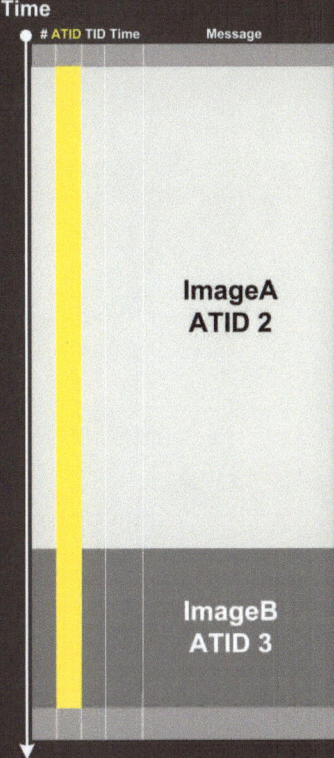

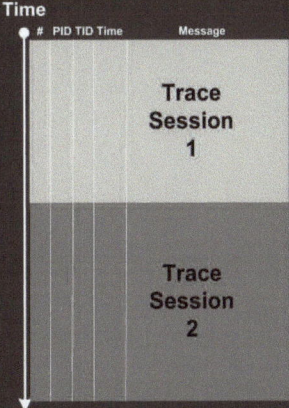

Examples here include log messages from different processes having the same **Adjoint Thread ID** such as the same operation name or network address. Another example is all messages coming from processes sharing the same name, or even, in general, periodic logging sessions appended to the end of the same log file.

Break-in Activity

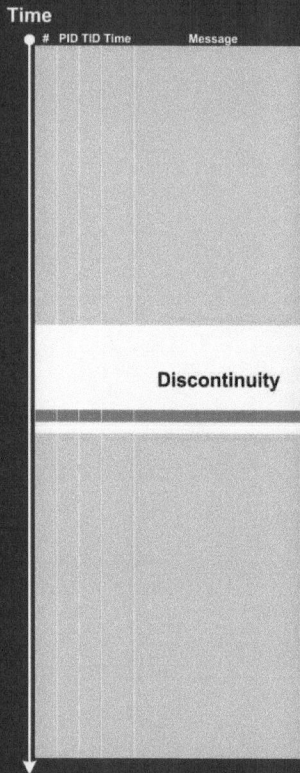

This pattern covers a message or a set of messages that surface just before the end of **Discontinuity** (a temporal gap) of some **Thread of Activity** or **Adjoint Thread**. For example, a silent process suddenly starts some network activity.

Data Flow

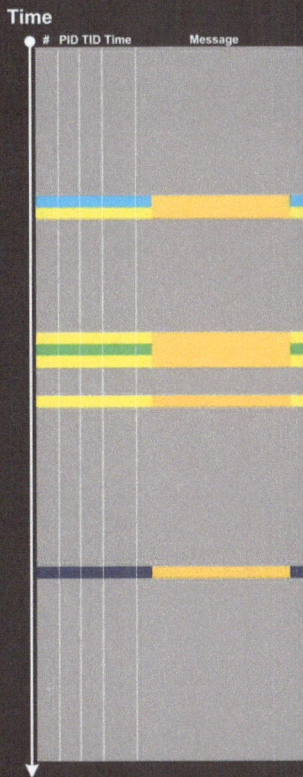

Time

PID TID Time   Message

If trace messages contain some character or formatted data that is passed from module to module or between threads and processes it is possible to trace that data and form a **Data Flow** thread similar to an **Adjoint Thread of Activity**. However, for **Data Flow** we may have completely different message types.

Message Patterns

- Significant Event
- Defamiliarizing Effect
- Anchor Messages
- Diegetic Messages
- Message Change
- Message Invariant
- UI Message
- Original Message
- Implementation Discourse
- Opposition Messages

- Linked Messages
- Gossip
- Counter Value
- Abnormal Value*
- Message Context
- Marked Messages
- Incomplete History
- Message Interleave
- Fiber Bundle

* added recently

© 2013 Software Diagnostics Services

The sixth block of patterns includes message patterns or patterns at the level of an individual message.

Significant Event

When looking at software traces and logs and doing either a search for or just scrolling certain messages have our attention immediately. We call them **Significant Events**. For malware analysis any suspicious message such as updating specific registry keys or creation of a popup window where we don't expect it would count as a significant event.

Defamiliarizing Effect

This pattern is about sudden unfamiliar trace statements across familiar landscape of **Characteristic Blocks** and **Activity Regions**. On the left we see familiar traces and on the right a new trace from an incident system.

Abnormal Value

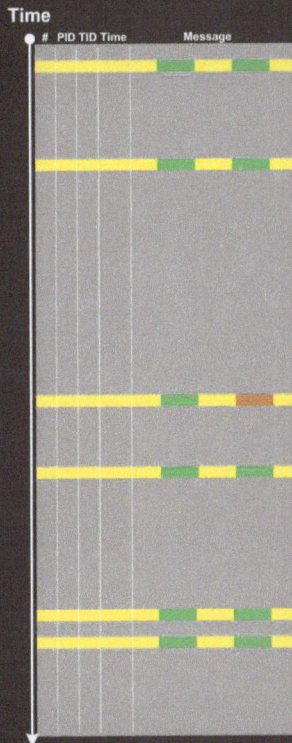

This pattern is about abnormal or unexpected values in a software trace or log such as a network address outside expected range.

Marked Messages

Annotated messages:

```
network activity [+]
process A launched [+]
process B launched [-]
process A exited [-]
```

[+] activity is present in a trace
[-] activity is undetected or not present

This pattern groups trace messages based on having some feature or property. For example, marked messages may point to some domain of software activity. Unmarked messages include all other messages that don't say anything about such activities or messages that say explicitly that no such activity has occurred. We can annotate any log after analysis to compare it with a **Master Trace** pattern (which is a normal expected trace corresponding to normal system).

Fiber Bundle

Trace
messages

I/O stack

Thread stack
trace

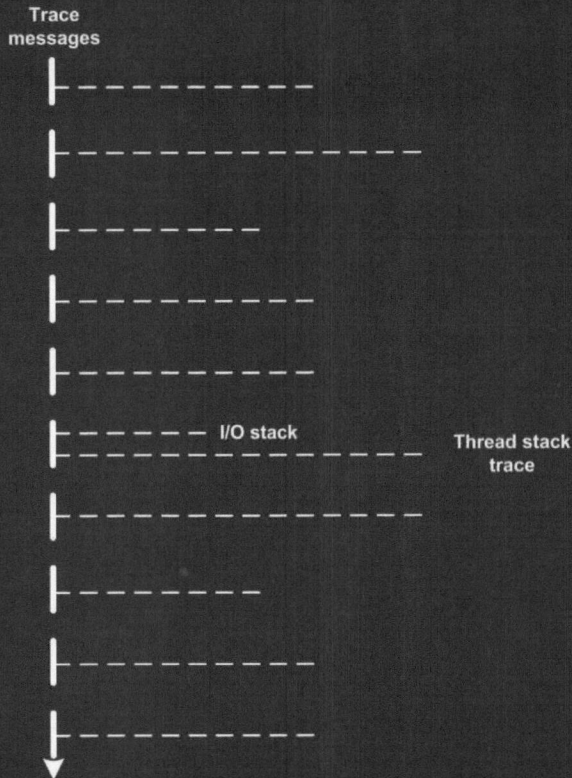

The modern software log recording, visualization and analysis tools provide stack traces associated with log messages. We can consider stack traces as software logs as well and, in a more general case, bundle them together (or attach as fibers) to a base software log. For example, a log message, that mentions an I/O request packet can have its I/O stack attached together with a thread stack trace with function calls leading to a function that emitted the log message.

The seventh block is about patterns related to message aggregates or message blocks.

Periodic Message Block

This is an obvious pattern, for example, a repeated network activity messages that are usually grouped together, so I don't provide any further comments here.

Trace Set Patterns

- Master Trace
- Bifurcation Point
- Inter-Correlation
- Relative Density
- News Value
- Impossible Trace
- Split Trace

The eighth block contains patterns for trace sets when we have several software logs.

Master Trace

© 2013 Software Diagnostics Services

When reading and analyzing software logs we always compare them to a **Master Trace** which is a standard log corresponding to normal, incident free use case.

Inter-Correlation

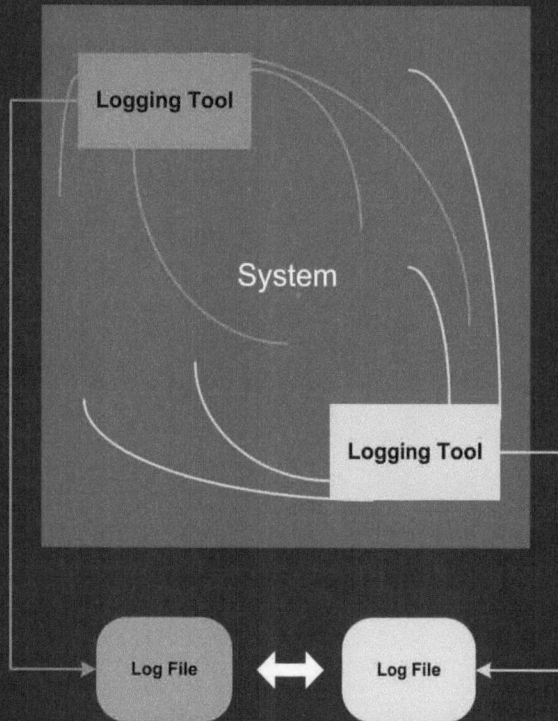

This pattern involves several logs from possibly different logging tools recorded (most commonly) at the same time or during an overlapping time interval. However, the purpose of using different logging tools is to cover events more completely. One of examples we can provide here is when we have a **Discontinuity**, a gap in one trace, and its interval events are covered by a different tool or we need to trace network activity more thoroughly in addition to file and registry activity.

Impossible Trace

```
#      Module  PID TID Message
--------------------------------
[…]
1001 ModuleA 202 404 foo: start
1002 ModuleA 202 404 foo: end
[…]
```

```
void foo()
{
    TRACE("foo: start");
    bar();
    TRACE("foo: end");
}

void bar()
{
    TRACE("bar: start");
    // some code ...
    TRACE("bar: end");
}
```

Although rarely (at least for myself) but it happens that when we look at an execution trace and then say it's an **Impossible Trace**. For example, we see on the trace fragment shown on the left of this slide that the function *foo* had been called. However, if we look at the corresponding source code on the right we would see that something is missing: the function *bar* must have been called with its own set of trace messages we don't see in the trace. Here we might suspect that the runtime code was being modified, perhaps by patching. We can also suspect local buffer overflows that led to a wrong return address skipping the code with expected tracing statements.

Grand Unification

- Narrative and Trace

$$N:\ T \to M$$

- Generalized Narrative and Trace

$$GN:\ A \to M$$

$$GN_3 \circ GN_2 \circ GN_1:\ M \to M \to M$$

Finally, we show a glimpse of what is forthcoming: a grand unification of software log and memory dump analysis through the so called generalized narrative. Usually a narrative is a temporal sequence of events and in the case of a software trace we can consider it as small memory fragments ordered by time. However, instead of time we can use any set as a domain of such mapping and even use memory itself and compose narratives together. I'll not talk more about it now.

Further Reading

- <u>Software Diagnostics Institute</u>
- <u>Memory Dump Analysis Anthology: Volumes 3, 4, 5, 6, ...</u>
  Volume 7 is in preparation (April, 2013)
  Volume 8 is planned for November, 2013
- <u>Introduction to Software Narratology</u>
- <u>Accelerated Windows Software Trace Analysis</u>

Here are some links for further reading. All log analysis patterns are briefly described on Software Diagnostics Institute web site. They are also available in edited form in Memory Dump Analysis Anthology volumes starting from volume 3. Also there is a recorded introduction to Software Narratology and even a 4 hour accelerated training course.

Software Diagnostics Institute:

http://www.dumpanalysis.org

Memory Dump Analysis Anthology volumes:

http://www.patterndiagnostics.com/ultimate-memory-analysis-reference

Introduction to Software Narratology:

http://www.patterndiagnostics.com/Introduction-Software-Narratology-materials

Accelerated Windows Software Trace Analysis:

http://www.patterndiagnostics.com/accelerated-windows-software-trace-analysis-book

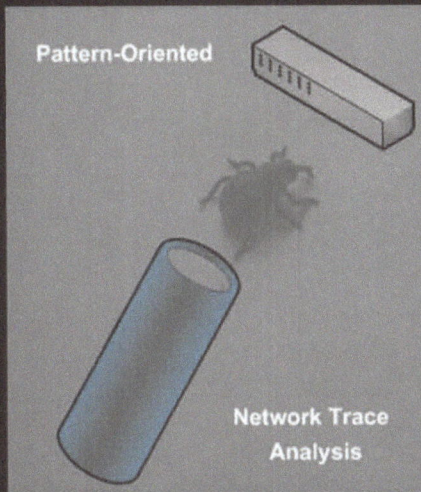

What's Next?

Pattern-Oriented

Network Trace
Analysis

Pattern-Oriented Network Trace Analysis

© 2013 Software Diagnostics Services

The next application of software narratology is network trace analysis. Please register for the forthcoming free webinar on our Software Diagnostics Services website.

Pattern-Oriented Network Trace Analysis:

http://www.patterndiagnostics.com/pattern-oriented-network-trace-analysis-materials

Network
Trace Analysis
Pattern-Oriented

Version 1.0

Dmitry Vostokov
Software Diagnostics Services

Published by OpenTask, Republic of Ireland

OpenTask books and magazines are available through booksellers and distributors worldwide. For further information or comments send requests to press@opentask.com.

A CIP catalogue record for this book is available from the British Library.

ISBN-l3: 978-1-908043-58-0 (Paperback)

First printing, 2013

Hello Everyone, my name is Dmitry Vostokov and I introduce today a software narratological approach to network trace analysis. I decided to keep this presentation short and as simple as possible. If anything needs to be added or modified in the future I create another version of it.

Facebook:
http://www.facebook.com/SoftwareDiagnosticsServices

Linkedin:
http://www.linkedin.com/company/software-diagnostics-services

Twitter:
http://twitter.com/DumpAnalysis

Wireshark

Hark

- Listen (to) *"Hark! There's the big bombardment."*
- Speak in one's ear; whisper

Shorter Oxford English Dictionary

Hark back *(idiom)*

- To return to a previous point, as in a narrative

http://www.thefreedictionary.com/hark

© 2013 Software Diagnostics Services

Before we start I'd like to offer an interpretation of Wireshark tool pronunciation. You see that it is connected with a notion of a narrative, a story. Why a narrative you see during this presentation.

Prerequisites

- Interest in software diagnostics, troubleshooting, debugging and network trace analysis

- Experience in network trace analysis using Wireshark or Network Monitor

Prerequisites for this presentation are very simple and I suppose you all like me enjoy diagnosing software problems and often going side-by-side network problems. I also assume that you already have experience in network trace analysis or at least familiarity with Wireshark interface. In such a case I hope this webinar outlines a unified pattern-oriented approach to network trace analysis in the context of general software trace analysis. If you only have experience in software log analysis but don't have any experience in network trace analysis it should provide a foundation for further study. A separate training course is coming soon too that will cover much more with detailed exercises. Originally I planned to add some demonstrations too but due to the time limit and size of this presentation (it grew up to almost 50 slides) I decided to omit them.

Why?

- A common diagnostics language

- Network diagnostics as software diagnostics

Why we advocate a general pattern approach to traditional network trace analysis? Because we need a unified language in the context of general software diagnostics and network trace analysis is largely a part of software diagnostics. As we would see later network trace structure and dynamics are similar to general software logs, for example, from Windows Process Monitor or from large scale software systems such as Citrix products which have their own tracing infrastructure based on Event Tracing for Windows.

Software Diagnostics

A discipline studying abnormal software structure and behavior in software execution artifacts (such as memory dumps, software and network traces and logs) using pattern-driven, systemic and pattern-based analysis methodologies.

© 2013 Software Diagnostics Services

First, I would like to remind you a definition of software diagnostics we put forward in one of our previous webinars. So you see that network trace analysis and associated software behavior fall under our definition of software diagnostics.

Pattern-driven:
http://www.patterndiagnostics.com/Introduction-Software-Diagnostics-materials

Systemic:
http://www.patterndiagnostics.com/systemic-diagnostics-materials

Pattern-based:
http://www.dumpanalysis.org/pattern-based-software-diagnostics

Diagnostics Pattern

A common recurrent identifiable problem together with **a set of recommendations** and **possible** solutions to apply in a specific context.

© 2013 Software Diagnostics Services

Next we would like to mention a definition of a software diagnostics pattern. There are some differences with a usual definition of a pattern from software construction such as architectural and design patterns. The difference is that often upon a diagnostic encounter we provide recommendations and possible solutions instead of just problem solutions. Recommendations may include immediate actions, for example, upon the detection of a significant amount of network traffic.

Pattern Orientation

Pattern-driven

- Finding patterns in software artefacts
- Using checklists and pattern catalogs

Pattern-based

- Pattern catalog evolution
- Catalog packaging and delivery

So you see that software diagnostics is about patterns and pattern recognition. Let's say it is pattern-oriented and includes pattern-based and pattern-driven parts. Pattern-driven is about diagnostics process and pattern-based is about pattern life cycle. We first start with the pattern-driven part.

Catalog Classification

- ⊚ **By abstraction**

  Meta-patterns

- ⊚ **By artifact type**

  Software Log*   Memory Dump   **Network Trace***

- ⊚ **By story type**

  Problem Description   Software Disruption   UI Problem

- ⊚ **By intention**

  Malware

In pattern-driven analysis we use pattern catalogs of pattern descriptions. Catalogs can be classified by abstraction, for example, as software diagnostics meta-patterns which are patterns of software diagnostics itself, by the type of software execution artifacts, such as software traces and logs, memory dumps and network traces, by story type, such as by problem descriptions, by software disruptions, and by user interface problems. Also we can separate patterns by intention such as malware (with unintentional patterns, the rest, all grouped as Victimware). In this presentation we only consider network traces as a subtype of software traces.

Meta-patterns:
http://www.dumpanalysis.org/blog/index.php/2012/06/09/patterns-of-software-diagnostics-part-1/

Software Log:
http://www.dumpanalysis.org/blog/index.php/trace-analysis-patterns/

Memory Dump:
http://www.dumpanalysis.org/blog/index.php/crash-dump-analysis-patterns/

Network Trace:
http://www.dumpanalysis.org/blog/index.php/2012/07/19/network-trace-analysis-patterns-part-1/

Problem Description:
http://www.dumpanalysis.org/blog/index.php/2012/03/11/software-problem-description-patterns-part-1/

Software Disruption:
http://www.dumpanalysis.org/blog/index.php/2013/01/12/software-disruption-patterns-part-1/

UI Problem:
http://www.dumpanalysis.org/blog/index.php/user-interface-problem-analysis-patterns/

Malware:
http://www.dumpanalysis.org/blog/index.php/malware-analysis-patterns/

Traces and Logs

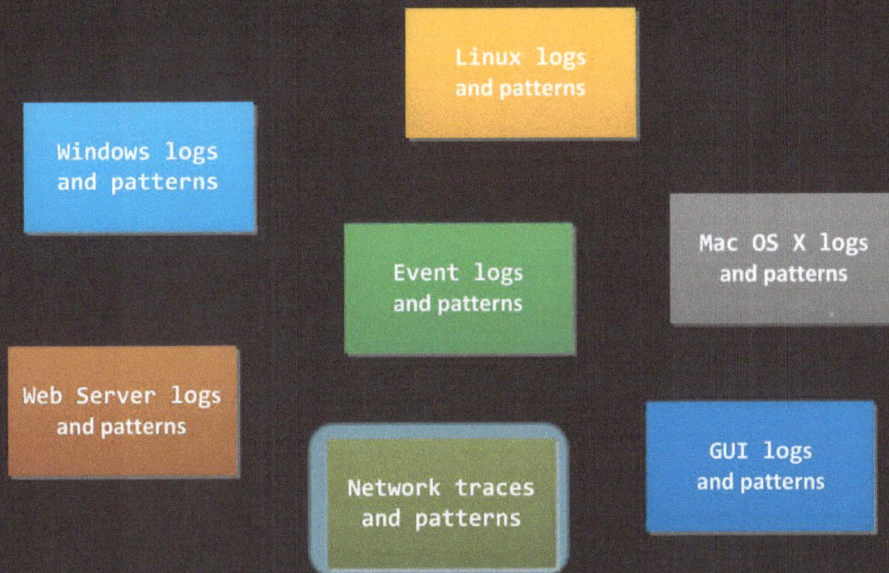

Linux logs and patterns

Windows logs and patterns

Mac OS X logs and patterns

Event logs and patterns

Web Server logs and patterns

Network traces and patterns

GUI logs and patterns

© 2013 Software Diagnostics Services

Software diagnostics analyses various software traces and logs. There are so many of them with different formats, OS and product specific information.

Trace and Log Patterns

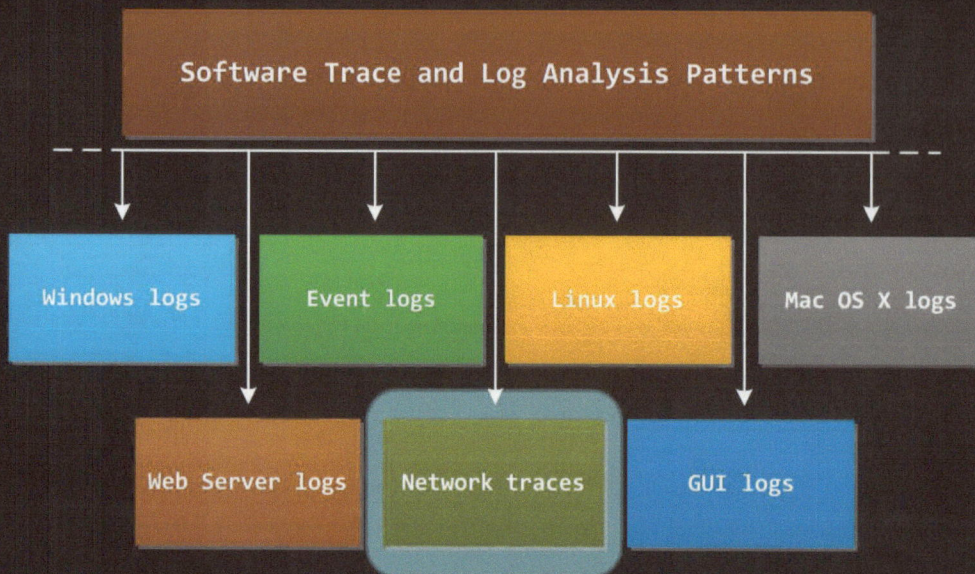

Software Trace and Log Analysis Patterns

Windows logs — Event logs — Linux logs — Mac OS X logs

Web Server logs — Network traces — GUI logs

© 2013 Software Diagnostics Services

A unifying approach was needed for a pattern catalog. The needed solution would use the common structure of all these logs and associated patterns. Initially we didn't consider network traces and added them as afterthought to make sense of them. Fortunately, software trace and log analysis patterns are applicable to network trace analysis because network traces can be considered as software narratives.

Software Narrative

A temporal sequence of events related to software execution.

The analysis of software narratives uses narratology, the discipline that studies various narrative forms such as stories, novels, chronicles, dialogues, because all these narratives have the same unified structure such as events ordered by time.

Software Trace

- A sequence of formatted messages
- Arranged by time
- A narrative story

For our purposes a software trace is just a sequence of formatted messages sent from running software, for example, an event log or intercepted and formatted API requests such as a log from Process Monitor tool or a network trace. They are usually arranged by time and can be considered as a software narrative story.

Network Trace

- A sequence of formatted packets as trace messages
- Arranged by time
- A narrative story

Network trace analysis is done on a packet level and packets can be considered as trace messages too. We analyze a network trace for any structural and behavioral patterns from a pattern catalogue.

By network trace analysis patterns we consider a subset of software trace and log analysis patterns because they all have the same underlying narratological structure.

Capture Tool Placing

- Sniffer placing

- Process Monitor placing

There are more similarities with a software trace analysis. For example, in a distributed environment we need to plan on what computers we should do our tracing.

The same goes for network and product deployment diagrams. It's good to have them before troubleshooting.

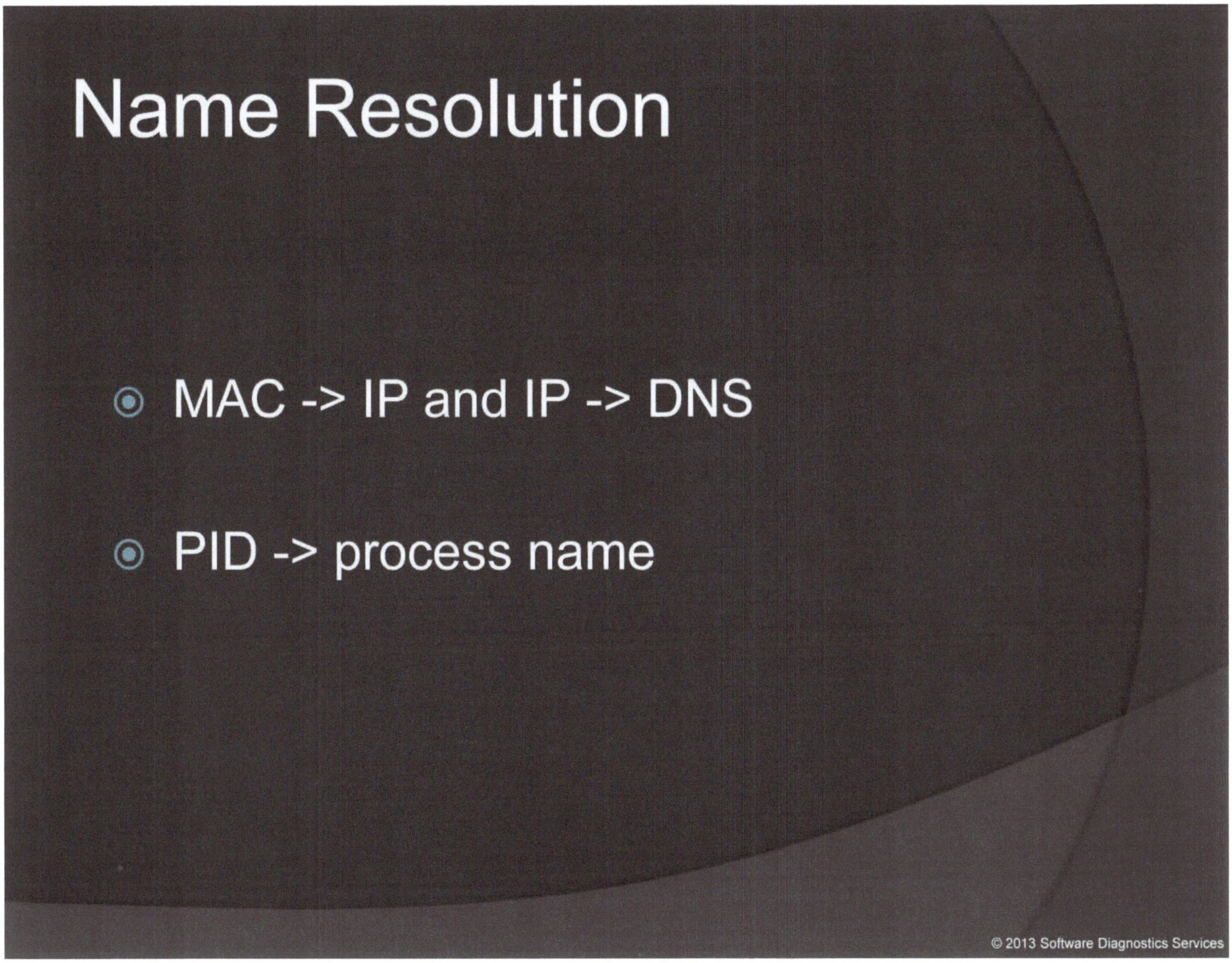

Name Resolution
MAC -> IP and IP -> DNS
PID -> process name
© 2013 Software Diagnostics Services

There are also parallels for better trace presentation such as converting data to human readable formats with added semantics. Presentation or trace representation is also a part of software narratology and narratology in general as we can see on the following slide I borrowed from the previous Software Narratology presentation.

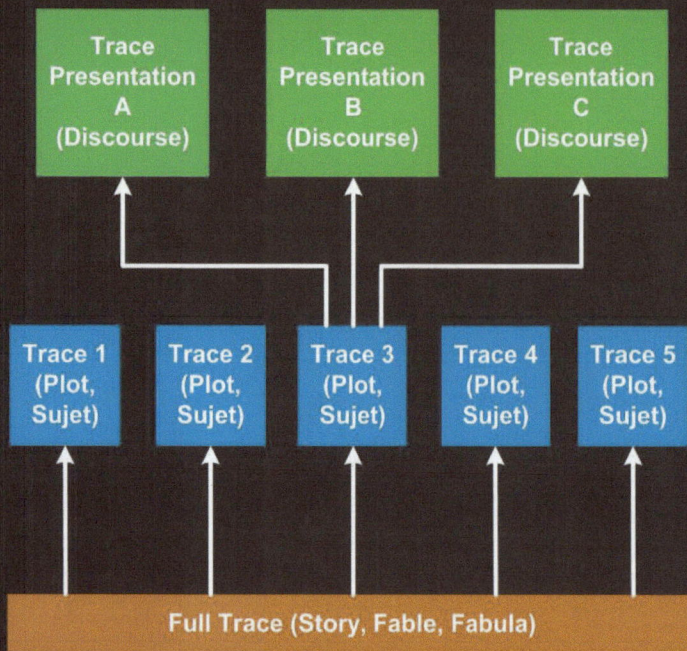

© 2013 Software Diagnostics Services

The events of the whole full story (also called a fable or fabula) can be rearranged in numerous ways to create various plots (with suspension as in fiction thrillers) also called sujets. Before or during network capture the tracing of certain packets can be switched off or on. When we analyze network traces we apply certain display filters in order to reduce their size. So we get different network plots or sujects from the possible full network story or fabula. But every individual plot can be presented differently, for example, in a novel or a poem, and even in a movie. The same goes for network software stories as well.

Minimal Trace Graphs

In order to illustrate network trace analysis patterns graphically we use the simplified abstracted pictorial representation of a typical software log. It has all essential features such as message number, time, endpoints and packet data itself.

Pattern-Driven Analysis

Logs → Checklists ↔ Patterns → Action

© 2013 Software Diagnostics Services

A few words about logs, checklists, and patterns. You probably have seen the same diagram in previous webinars and trainings. This is an essential feature of pattern-driven software diagnostics. Software trace analysis is usually an analysis of a formatted text for the presence of patterns. Here checklists can be very useful.

Pattern-Based Analysis

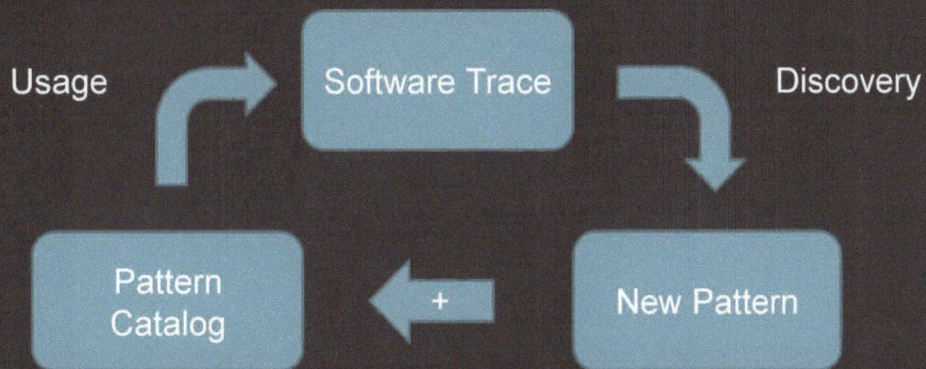

Usage → Software Trace → Discovery

Software Trace → New Pattern

New Pattern + → Pattern Catalog

Pattern Catalog → Software Trace

© 2013 Software Diagnostics Services

Pattern catalogs are rarely fixed. New patterns are constantly discerned or refined. For example, while preparing this webinar I found yet another missing pattern for network conversations and added it to the trace analysis pattern catalog. It became useful not only for network trace analysis but also for window message logs and multi-computer traces.

Pattern Classification

- Vocabulary
- Error
- Trace as a Whole
- Large Scale
- Activity
- Message
- Block
- Trace Set

Recently all software trace and log analysis patterns (which are now numbered more than 70 at the time of this writing) were classified into several categories. Vocabulary category consists of patterns related to problem description. Error category covers general error distribution patterns. This classification also considers traces as wholes, their large scale structure, activity patterns, patterns related to individual trace message structure, patterns related to collection of messages (the so called blocks) and finally patterns related to several traces and logs as a collection of artifacts from a software incident. Because network trace analysis is only a part of general software diagnostics and we just started exploring network narratives we selected only a few patterns from these categories as relevant to illustrate our software narratological approach.

Reference and Course

- ◉ Catalog from Software Diagnostics Library

  Software Trace Analysis Patterns

- ◉ Free reference graphical slides

  Accelerated-Windows-Software-Trace-Analysis-Public.pdf

- ◉ Training course*

  Accelerated Windows Software Trace Analysis

  * Available as a full color paperback book, PDF book, on SkillsSoft Books 24x7. Recording is available for all book formats

© 2013 Software Diagnostics Services

Most patterns are very intuitive if you analyse network traces and software logs in general. Here I provided a few links for general software trace and log analysis used as a foundation for pattern-oriented network trace analysis. After you download a presentation you can follow these links.

Software Trace Analysis Patterns:
http://www.dumpanalysis.org/blog/index.php/trace-analysis-patterns/

Free reference graphical slides:
http://www.patterndiagnostics.com/Training/Accelerated-Windows-Software-Trace-Analysis-Public.pdf

Training course:
http://www.patterndiagnostics.com/accelerated-software-trace-analysis

Selected Patterns

Now I present a few selected patterns with diagrams.

Master Trace

Normal network capture

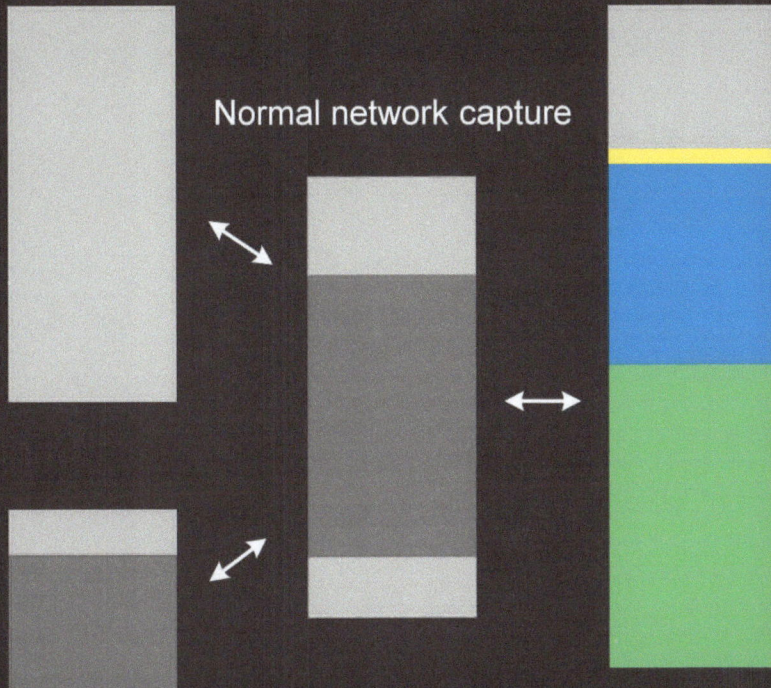

© 2013 Software Diagnostics Services

When reading and analyzing network traces and logs we always compare them to a **Master Trace** which is a standard or normal network capture.

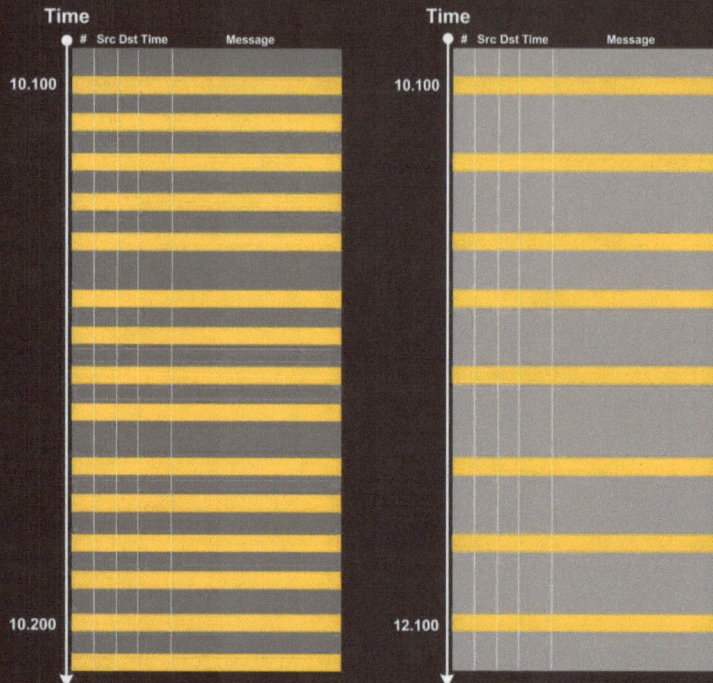

Message Current

$J_1 > J_2$

Packets/s

© 2013 Software Diagnostics Services

Message Current (also called Statement Current) is the number of messages per unit of time. This is similar to velosity, first-order derivative. A trace can also be partitioned into **Activity Regions** with different currents and current can also be measured between significant trace events.

Message Density

$$D_1 > D_2$$

© 2013 Software Diagnostics Services

The statement or message density is simply the ratio of the number of occurrences of the specific trace statement (message) in the trace to the total number of all different recorded messages.

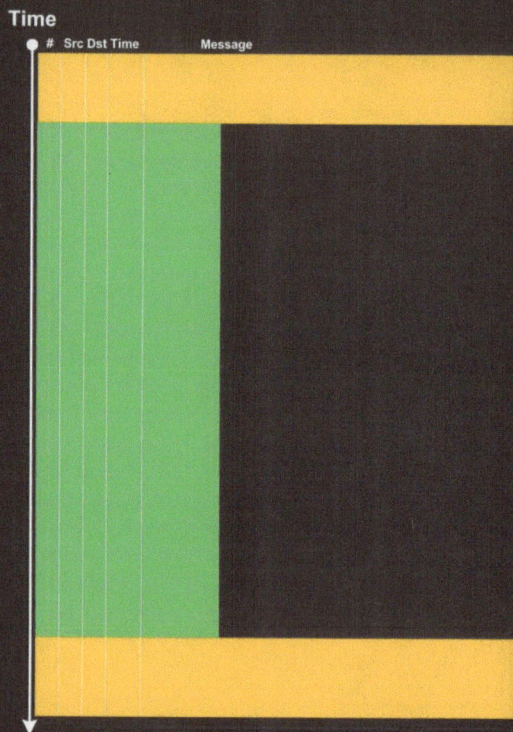

Message part can be variable and despite less density certain endpoints may generate more byte traffic. The full name of this pattern is **Characteristic Message Block** and originally it was devised for irregularities of formatting and here payload length may serve well but generally any characteristic function can be applied.

Example

All the latter patterns can be seen in Conversations dialog in Wireshark.

Thread of Activity

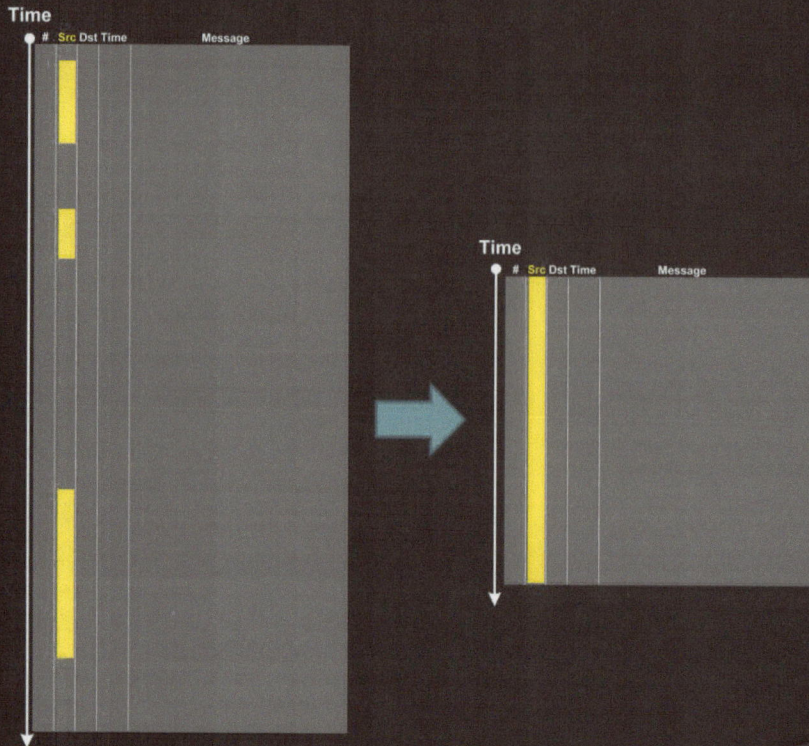

In software trace analysis **Thread of Activity** pattern usually means trace messages associated with the particular Thread ID. Usually when we see an error indication or some interesting message we select its current thread and investigate what happened in this process and thread before. By looking at threads we can also spot discontinuities. In network trace analysis we can select a source as a thread, for example.

Adjoint Thread

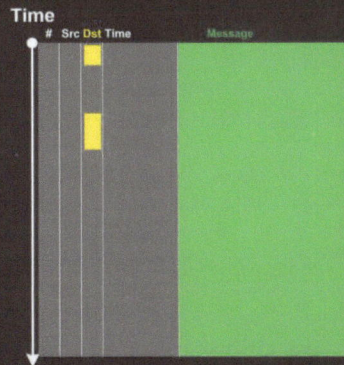

Time

Pattern Category

Activity

Filtered by:

- ◉ Source
- ◉ Destination
- ◉ Protocol
- ◉ Message
- ◉ Expression

If a thread is a linear ordered flow of activities associated with particular Thread ID or Source as seen from trace message perspective through time we can also extend this flow concept and consider a linear flow of activities associated with some other parameter such as Destination, Protocol, Message or some expression. Such trace messages may have different Thread IDs or sources associated with them but also some chosen constant parameter or column value in a trace viewing tool. The name **adjoint** comes from the fact that in threads of activity Thread ID or Source stays the same but other message attributes vary but in adjoint threads we have the opposite.

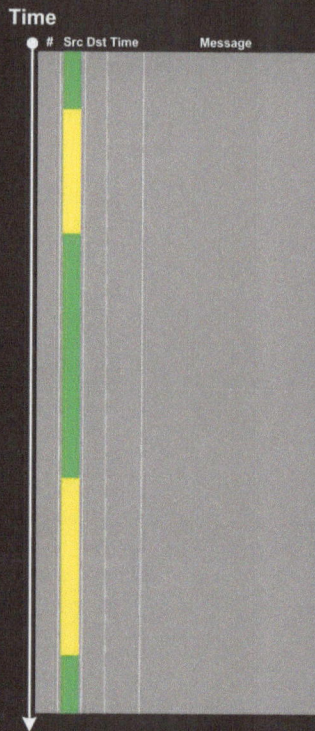

No Activity

Time

#	Src	Dst	Time	Message

We messages from other servers but only see our own traffic

No Activity is an obvious pattern when we don't see any expected trace messages. It could also be the case of endpoints or protocols not selected for tracing. It is a limit of the next pattern called **Discontinuity**.

Discontinuity

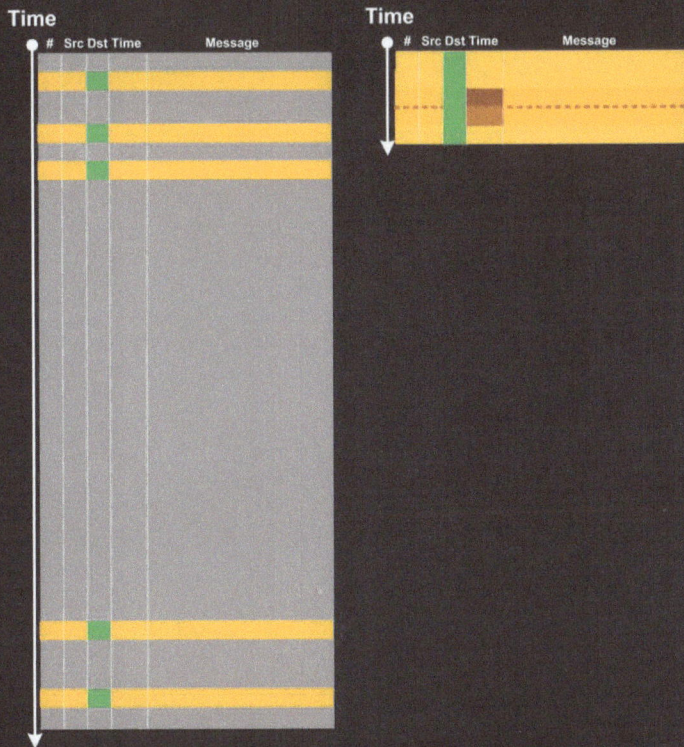

This pattern is about delays. When we select **Thread of Activity** or **Adjoint Thread of Activity** we see such delays better.

Dialog

Conversation between 2 endpoints

© 2013 Software Diagnostics Services

Dialogue is an important pattern especially in network trace analysis. It usually involves a message source, a different message target (although both can be the same) and some alternation between them as shown on this abstract trace diagram. This pattern was added recently and has not yet been classified.

Significant Event

Time

Time Reference feature in Wireshark

When looking at a network trace and doing search for or just scrolling certain messages have our attention immediately. We call them **Significant Events**. The start of a trace and the end of it are trivial significant events and are used in deciding whether the trace is **Circular**, and also in determining the trace recording interval (**Time Delta** pattern) or its average **Message Current**. Some significant messages can be used as a time reference too.

Marked Messages

Annotated messages:

```
session initialization [+]
session tear-off [-]
port A activity [+]
port B activity [-]
protocol C used [-]
address D used [-]
```

Marked Packets
feature in Wireshark

[+]   activity is present in a trace
[-]   activity is undetected or not present

This pattern groups trace messages based on having some feature or property. For example, marked messages may point to some network activity and therefore may help in troubleshooting and debugging. Unmarked messages include all other messages that don't say anything about such activities (although may include messages pointing to such activities indirectly we unaware of) or messages that say explicitly that no such activity has occurred. We can annotate any trace or log after analysis to compare it with a **Master Trace** pattern (which is a normal expected network trace). Sometimes a non-present activity can be a marked activity corresponding to all inclusive unmarked present activity (for example, **No Activity** pattern). Some tools such as Wireshark allow you to mark specific trace messages to help in analysis.

Partition

Here we introduce a software narratological (like a software story) partitioning of a network trace into **Head**, **Prologue**, **Core**, **Epilogue** and **Tail** segments. Some elements such as **Head** and **Tail** may be optional and combined with **Prologue** and **Epilogue**. This is useful for comparative network trace analysis. Please note that such partitioning can be done for any filtered trace such as **Adjoint Thread of Activity**.

This pattern involves several traces from possibly different network trace tools recorded (most commonly) at the same time or during an overlapping time interval or a combination of a network trace with some other trace or log such as from Process Monitor. The purpose of using different tracing tools is to cover events more completely.

Circular Trace

Pattern Category

Trace as a Whole

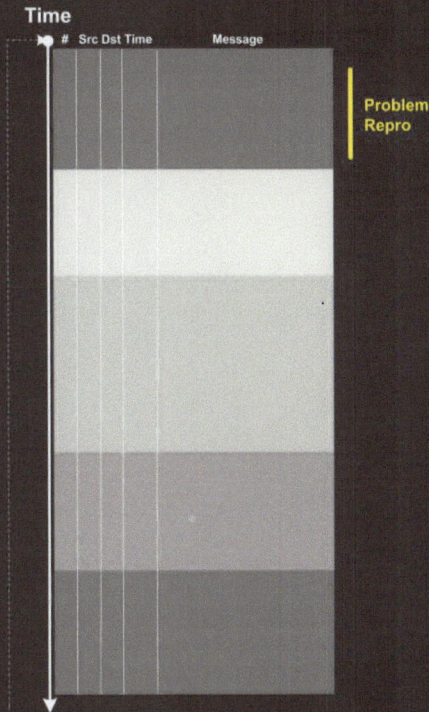

One of common problems with tracing are rare and non-reproducible incidents. If the amount of traffic is small per second it is possible to record events for hours or days. However if we need to trace all communication as to do filtering later then trace files can grow uncontrollable. Some tools enable circular tracing and after reaching particular file size the tracing stream overwrites older messages.

Split Trace

Time

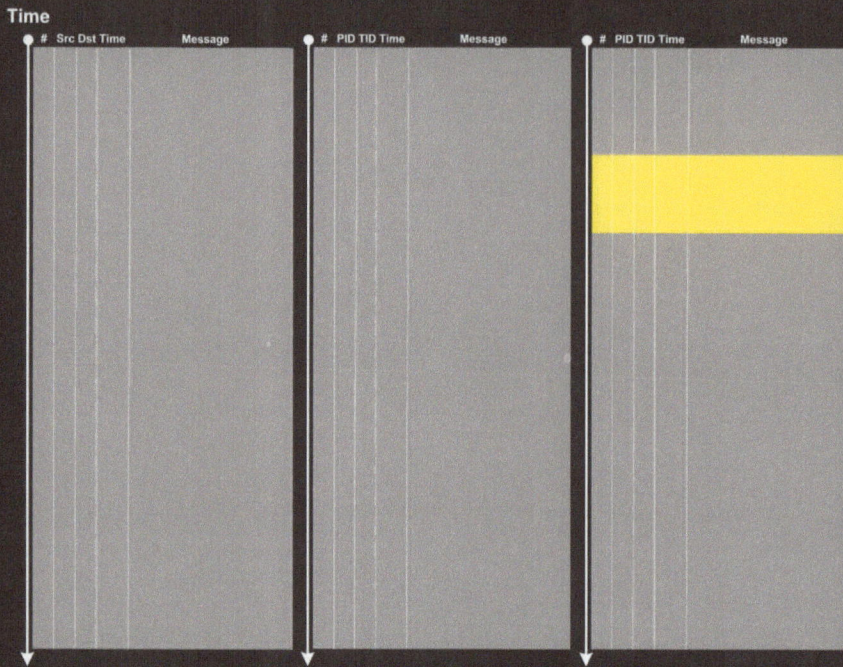

Some network tracing tools such as Wireshark have an option to split network traces into several files during long capture. Although this should be done judiciously it is really necessary sometimes.

Additional useful concept from narratology is a concept of a paratext. This is additional information about a text useful for its interpretation such as a book cover, an introduction from an editor, notes or the list of other referenced texts. This is not a pattern yct and will be added to the catalogue soon.

Frames

Time

Src Dst Time   Message

OSI, TCP/IP Layers

© 2013 Software Diagnostics Services

Frames pattern can describe various protocol layers.

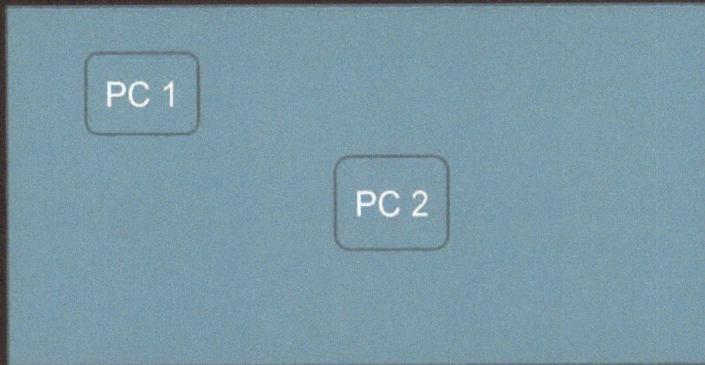

Sometimes due to network configuration or sniffer placement some computers will be excluded and their traffic will not be seen in a trace. In the context of a general software trace **Visibility Tracing** pattern means impossibility of logging some functionality, for example, before the tracing subsystem or service starts.

Due to a packet loss we may have an incomplete tracing history. Missing responses or acknowledgements are also covered by this pattern.

Possible New Patterns

- Full Trace (promiscuous mode)

- Embedded Message (PDU chain, protocol data unit, packet)

- Ordered Message (TCP/IP sequence numbers)

- Illegal Message (sniffed with illegally obtained privileges)

- Dual Trace (in / out, duplex)

On this slide we list an incomplete list of some possible patterns we plan to evaluate and add in the future to our trace analysis pattern catalogue.

Further Reading

- Practical Packet Analysis, 2nd edition, by Chris Sanders

- Software Diagnostics Institute

- Memory Dump Analysis Anthology: Volumes 3, 4, 5, 6, ...
  Volume 7 is in preparation (July, 2013)

- Introduction to Software Narratology

- Malware Narratives

© 2013 Software Diagnostics Services

So we have covered a few selected patterns. Here are some links for further reading. On top we list a wonderful book especially useful for beginners in network trace analysis. The rest are links including to 2 other presentations on software trace analysis: *Introduction to Software Narratology* and *Malware Narratives*.

Software Diagnostics Institute:

http://www.dumpanalysis.org

Memory Dump Analysis Anthology volumes:

http://www.patterndiagnostics.com/ultimate-memory-analysis-reference

Introduction to Software Narratology:

http://www.patterndiagnostics.com/Introduction-Software-Narratology-materials

Malware Narratives:

http://www.patterndiagnostics.com/malware-narratives-materials

What's Next?

- Accelerated Network Trace Analysis

- Generative Software Narratology

- Pattern-Oriented Hardware Signal Analysis

© 2013 Software Diagnostics Services

The next application of software narratology we plan is hardware analysis. We also plan to extend software narratology to its generative form to include a layer of source code. We also plan training similar to *Accelerated Windows Software Trace Analysis* we developed last year. It is called *Accelerated Network Trace Analysis* and will have hands-on exercises for Wireshark and Network Monitor or possibly its successor Message Analyzer if it is released by that time. This training will also cover all applicable trace analysis patterns from our catalogue.

Generative Software Narratology:
http://www.patterndiagnostics.com/introduction-generative-software-narratology